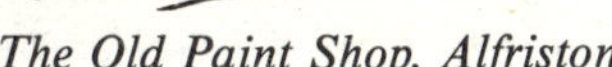
The Old Paint Shop, Alfriston.

Around Historic Sussex

Third edition

Drawings by Gerald Lip

EAGLE PUBLISHING COMPANY

The School House, Bodiam.

The superbly illustrated pen and ink drawings by Gerald Lip contained in this informative and easily read book have been selected from a series which has appeared in the Evening Argus every Friday for the past 17 years.

Gerald Lip was educated at Harrow School of Art and exhibited at the Royal Academy at a very early age, he is now cartoon editor of a well known national newspaper group. He was also art instructor at Army College North, Welbeck Abbey during his stint in the army. Much of his work has appeared in national newspapers and magazines throughout the years. Gerald Lip lives with his wife and young daughter in Hove.

First published in 1986 by
EAGLE PUBLISHING COMPANY
63b Lansdowne Place, Hove, Sussex.

ISBN 0 905782 10 0.

TO MUM + TED
SEPTEMBER
1986

ALL THE BEST
FOR THE FUTURE

Peter

The Anglers' Rest, Barcombe Mills

FOREWORD

by Terry Page

Editor, Brighton Evening Argus

Evening Argus

89 North Road
Brighton BN1 4AU
Tel: Brighton 606799

THE SOUTHERN PUBLISHING COMPANY (WESTMINSTER PRESS LIMITED)

Although I have only recently moved to Sussex, I have been a regular visitor to this most delightful county since schooldays 25 years ago. One of the greatest bargains at the time was to buy an early morning workman's rail ticket which cost four shillings and sixpence for the return journey from London to Brighton. Cycling here was my other great joy.

So as an old Sussex friend and a new resident I read with interest any book on the county. It is an added pleasure for this book to be illustrated with Gerald Lip's detailed drawings, which have been admired by my newspaper's readers for so long.

Terry Page

Contents and Illustrations

Saxon Cottage, Steyning.

Ghyll Manor, Rusper.

Brickwall House, Northiam.

Alciston

The sweetly-named Rose Cottage Inn, at Alciston, is believed to date from the early 17th century. Deeds for the flint and chalk-built pub survive back to October 30, 1800, when the property was sold by Viscount Gage to a George Liggatt.

In 1856 the building was divided into two cottages, and shortly afterwards was bought by a Mr A. Thorneycroft and converted into a public house and village shop. Photographs of the pub survive from the 1890's.

In the summer of 1898, the Rose Cottage pub was sold to the Southdown and East Grinstead breweries and in 1924 was transferred to the Tamplins brewery of Brighton.

In 1971 the pub was purchased from the brewery by the Lewis family, who had been tenants for 12 years previously.

Alfriston

Alfriston's medieval thatched Clergy House enjoys a beautiful setting on the outskirts of the village.

This charming, timber-framed building was built around 1350 for the use of parish priests.

It dates from a critical stage in English history, just after the two-year period when the Black Death had decimated the country's population from four million to two and a half million.

At the time, half of the land in the country was untilled and many manor houses ruined or abandoned. So, seen in this light, the construction of a Clergy House was obviously a high priority of the time – or perhaps Alfriston was an unusually rich parish.

The Clergy House, true to its name, was built as a dwelling for priests. After the Reformation, when clergy were permitted to marry, the house became the vicarage for St. Andrew's Church.

Around 1790, the house ceased to be the vicarage and was converted into two farm labourers' cottages.

In 1885, the local vicar, who was entitled to the rent, decided the building was so dilapidated he applied to the church for permission to demolish the building. This was agreed.

But the destruction of this lovely medieval house was saved for two reasons. The existing tenant, an old woman, begged to be able to stay in the house, which she did until her death in 1888.

Then in 1889, a new vicar, the Rev F. W. Benyon, was appointed to the St. Andrew's parish – and immediately recognised the historical importance of the building.

For seven years, he fought to save the house, often doing temporary repair work with his own hands. In 1892 he launched an appeal for £450, but this had only produced £124 by February 1893.

But the National Trust was formed in 1894, and in February 1896, the Clergy House became only the second property to come under its care.

Alfriston

The Market Cross pub in Alfriston, better known as The Smugglers, was once owned by one of the village's most notable – and disreputable – inhabitants.

Stanton Collins, the leader of the Alfriston gang of smugglers in the nineteenth century, lived there.

The pub has numerous corridors leading to 21 rooms, 48 doors and six staircases. There are also various secret hiding places and exits to the stables at the rear.

The secret niches and exits were built to give the smugglers a quick escape, but they have now been sealed up.

A room at the back of the house was used by the Alfriston gang as their headquarters. it has five doors, two of them leading to the stables and outhouses where Collins kept his horses and stored his smuggled goods.

The pub stands beside the Market Cross of Alfriston itself. The cross is thought to have been built in about 1405 when Henry IV granted to "the King's town of Alfryston" the right to hold a market weekly on Tuesday, and two annual fairs.

The original cross stood until November 1955, but it was badly damaged. It was replaced by a round cap shaped like a shepherd's crown in about 1830.

Twice this century the shaft of the original cross has been broken. Once was in 1955, when a lorry crashed into it.

The ancient stone steps have also been removed. They were taken out in the nineteenth century because they obstructed traffic, and replaced by a brick base.

The large stones now at the base of the cross are portions of the mullions of windows from the church, removed during restoration work during the 1870s and 80s.

Alfriston

The Star of Bethlehem has always been the pub sign of the charming Star Inn at Alfriston. It was founded in the 13th century by the monks of Battle Abbey as a hostel for pilgrims on their way to worship at the shrine of St. Richard at Chichester.

The present heavily-timbered building dates from 1450, the year Jack Cade led his ill-fated rebellion out of Kent – and the year before the English were chased out of all their French lands, apart from Calais.

Around that time, the Star shared with churches the reputation as a place of refuge for people fleeing from justice. Inside the pub can still be seen the sanctuary post which the fugitives had to reach. They then had ten days grace before the chase was allowed to begin again.

This inn is roofed with massive slabs of Horsham stone, while the front exterior features many remarkable examples of medieval heraldic and religious wood carvings, including St. Michael in combat with a dragon. A grotesque carved figure of a lion which stands outside was taken from a Dutch ship wrecked off the coast in the 17th century.

The present bar, with a great Tudor fireplace and Sussex ironwork, was once the kitchen, while the upper storey is faced in plaster with upright timbering, and three lead-lighted windows. The Star is believed to be one of England's oldest inns, and the period architecture, in its picturesque village setting, has been carefully preserved.

Alfriston

The Lincoln handicap winner of 1912 was trained at the Wingrove House racing stables in the picturesque village of Alfriston.

The success was marked by a framed picture of the winning horse, which can still be seen in what is now the Wingrove restaurant.

Built in the early 19th century, the property was designed in colonial style. It has a slated roof, and a large ornate covered balcony on the first floor.

In its heyday, Wingrove used to lie in 196 acres of land, which included stabling for 32 horses, a grass paddock and training ground on the South Downs.

During the 20th century, the land was sold off bit by bit, and the stables converted into mews cottages, which still adjoin Wingrove.

It was during the 1930s that Wingrove House was converted into a hotel and restaurant.

Until recently, Wingrove was known as the Potter's Wheel, but new owners have restored the original name.

Wingrove restaurant enjoys pleasing views over the surrounding Downs, and diners overlook Alfriston's parish church, known as the "Cathedral of the South Downs," as well as an adjoining 14th century clergy house, which was the first building acquired by the National Trust in 1896.

Arundel

Arundel Town Hall once stood out from other large buildings in the town for one major reason – there was a giant swallow perched on its roof.

But the bird was not a refugee from a Hitchcock movie, just a wooden replica of the real thing, and it existed as the symbol of the town.

In 1978 it became apparent that things were not well with the swallow, for the ravages of time and the weather left him likely to topple from his perch. So, before the wood rotted completely, the famous Arundel swallow was taken down.

It was then that a local company director offered to replace the bird with a fibreglass replica, cast at his factory.

Unfortunately the bird has not yet been finished, so Arundel looks set to wait a little longer before the Town Hall can once again boast of having the town' symbol on top.

The original swallow was rescued from Arundel's old Swallow Brewery which was demolished after World War One.

The Town Hall itself was built in 1836 and the deed of covenance was executed in June 1848. Planners originally wanted to build on the site of the old Court House, but that involved demolishing several adjoining properties.

One owner, however, refused to sell, and the council rather huffily had to settle for the Maltravers Street site.

Arundel

Rampaging soldiers smashed up the front of the Castle Inn on Arundel Square. Beams were ripped from the front of the early Tudor building as the soldiers under Cromwell headed for the castle.

The building, now the Old Crown Inn restaurant and three shops, has a Queen Anne front and windows as a result of that destruction.

The premises were built as a coaching house around 1500. A large hall was built on in the 1800s for dances. The hall, with its oak flooring, fell into disrepair and was pulled down in 1974 and the area was turned into a car park.

When the Old Crown Inn restaurant changed hands, the new owners uncovered the beams and stripped 21 layers of wallpaper from the walls.

If the weather is damp it is still possible to see the word "Crown" painted on the stone along the top of the building.

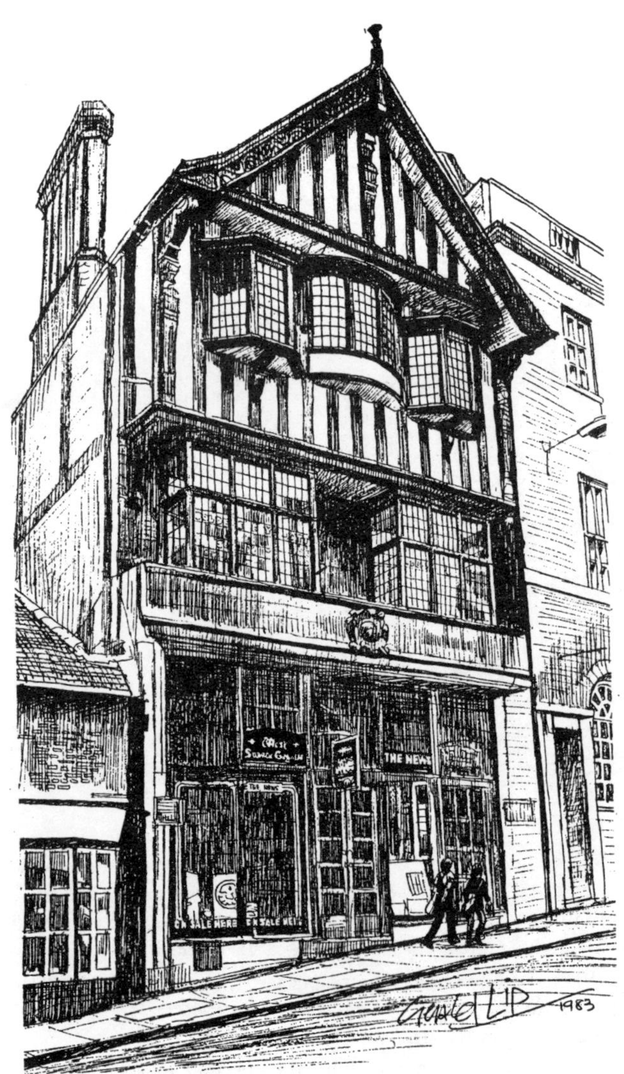

Arundel

When the owners of the West Sussex Gazette offices in Arundel decided to re-build, they were determined their new premises would blend in with the character of the town.

The architects, Wheeler and Lodge, of London and Horsham, armed with that brief settled on an adaptation of the typical Sussex half timber design.

The building was constructed in the Jacobean style with overhanging gable, carved oak brackets, projecting bays and lead glazed windows.

Built in 1900 the property drew praise from the magazine, The British Architect, who described it as, "the most artistic country newspaper office to be found in England."

It replaced a building which less than a decade earlier had been badly damaged by fire.

That building had seen the birth of the paper, although by the turn of the century the frontage was little more than a shell.

Despite new presses and printing machinery, the building itself was not up to the task of competing in a fast developing industry.

Ashurst Wood

The oldest sitting room in Britain is reputedly in Stoke Brunswick preparatory school, Ashurst Wood, East Grinstead.

The west wing of the school dates from the 14th century and was once used as the hunting lodge of the fourth son of Edward III, the powerful nobleman, John of Gaunt.

The lodge survives to form part of the headmaster's quarters at the school, where Winston Churchill was a former pupil.

The larger part of this attractive mellow-stone building dates from Tudor times and has an unusual history in that it was transported, brick by brick, from Cheshire.

In 1900, what is now Stoke Brunswick came into the hands of the Dewar family, of whisky fame, and in 1934 it was decided the house needed enlarging.

John Dewar's wife saw a photograph in a London bookshop of Dutton Manor, the seat of the Lords of Dutton in 1539. As it matched the Sussex building, the Dewars travelled to Cheshire, where they found the magnificent mansion reduced to a working farmhouse.

A deal was struck with the farmer, and Dutton Manor was dismantled beam by beam and brought south by steam lorry. Here it was skilfully re-erected with little regard to cost, and its rotten beams were replaced with ones from the Navy's last wooden ship, HMS Arethusa.

Stoke Brunswick School was formerly known as Brunswick School in Hove but moved to the present building in 1958.

In 1965, the school merged with Stoke House School, which had premises in Seaford.

Balcombe

Balcombe House, once the residence of Leonard Messel, grandfather of Lord Snowdon, is an old house set in a village steeped in history.

It was once called Parsonage House, with the first stone laid in March 1760, and its walls are 18 inches thick. Writing in the parish register at the time, the Rector of Balcombe, the Rev Richard Gawler Mead describes the building as "exceedingly strong and well built."

He was evidently very impressed with the building, for a few sentences later he says of the roof: "It is one of the finest that ever was framed."

But most Balcombe residents would find nothing strange in Mr Gawler's adulation of the area – they have known for years that it is one of the nicest places to live in Sussex.

The village lies 17 miles north of Brighton, four from Cuckfield and 33 from London.

The landscape is of gentle, wooded hills and tranquil streams flowing down to the Ouse. In a valley to the east is the picturesque Hammer Pond much frequented by fishermen.

The village itself exudes an air of weathered maturity. The church of St. Mary is constructed in stone and has mixed architectural styles.

In the area there are health springs and quarries that used to provide stone for the parish and neighbourhood, and once something of more immediate value was discovered in the area.

On May 24, 1897, a metal pot holding 12 gold and 742 silver coins was uncovered in the village – and quickly claimed by the Crown as treasure trove.

Balcombe

Balcombe is fortunate enough to lie in one of the greenest, quietest parts of Sussex, with a backdrop of gentle wooded hills and tranquil streams.

It boasts a wealth of attractive buildings, lush farmland and in a valley to the east lies a beautiful lake, once a hammer pond. One of the oldest properties in the village is Bretts Cottage on the Haywards Heath Road, which was built between 1400 and 1450.

Its name derives from a resident there in the 18th century, Sir William Brett, who was one of the Iron Masters of the period. The iron industry was once of paramount importance in that part of Sussex, and some believe the village derived its name from that trade.

That belief stems from the old village sign, an incandescent iron bal (old English for ball) emanating from a combe, which was a hollow on the flank of a hill.

Others believe that the name of the village came from a powerful local family, who later emigrated to the United States, where they are still well known.

Whatever the origins of the place, it has enjoyed a wealth of different spellings, ranging from the present form through Balcome, Bawcom and Bawcombe.

Balcombe

It's hard to believe, looking at the Mill House in Balcombe today, that anyone actually decided the place wasn't fit for them to live in.

But that's just what one family decided about the turn of the century, and promptly built a house in the village which they moved into in 1903.

They kept the old mill, but the separate mill house was sold. The mill itself continued to grind corn until about 1926.

The mill house property was built in about 1666 and probably consisted of a large dining room with cooking facilities on an inglenook fire with two bedrooms on the upper storey.

Eventually modern life caught up with the property, and a granary to the south of the house was joined to the main part to form a separate kitchen.

In about 1880 the miller built two rooms on the end of the house, which were used by the son and his bride when they were married soon after.

After the mill lost its connection with grinding corn in the 1920s, the parts were moved to Ifield Mill, which was in the process of being restored.

Battle

The Old Pharmacy in the heart of Battle was built in the late 15th century, and has probably been used as a shop for most of its long life.

It is a two-bay timber-framed Wealden style hall house, occupying a prime site in the centre of Battle High Street.

It was modernised in 1600, when the floor level was reset, and again in the early 18th century, and the building has been altered considerably over the years.

During Victorian times, the external beams were covered with a plaster facade, which was not removed until after World War Two.

Deeds of 1772 indicate the building was a long-established shop at that time, although it was once used by a brazier.

In the 1800s there was a schoolroom at the back of the shop.

The premises have been run as a chemist's shop since 1840. In addition to traditional medicines, groceries, musical instruments and even gunpowder were sold in the past.

A Finnish man, Karl Henry Emeleus, took over the business in 1903 from a pharmacist named William Harold.

The shop has also been extended into an adjoining building, dating from the 18th century.

Battle

The Priory House, at Battle, has concealed many costly secrets in its time. For the wool merchant who used to own the house in the 1700s was reputed to have been "banker" for wealthy people in the local area.

He would store valuables entrusted to him concealed in the chimney breast on the second floor, which has a hinged panel over the fireplace.

Priory House, which became a hotel 22 years ago, is a three-storey building, attractive apple green plaster and wood frontage dates from the Queen Anne period of 1700.

In the tiled roof are dormer windows with pediments and a heavy, square chimney stack of brick, with panelled faces and moulded cornice. The cornice bears the date 1700 in large metal figures.

At the eaves, is a wooden entableture with egg and tongue ornament, enriched brackets and moulded cornice.

The middle doorway has a moulded architrave and a flat hood carrying a balcony.

The chief feature inside Priory House is an oak staircase, which except for the lower flight now removed, rises to the top floor.

There is another serpentine staircase from the first floor to the ground floor.

Bodiam

Justin's at Bodiam, was once used as a German prisoner-of-war-camp.

It was built by a Mr Levett and two farm labourers between 1911 and 1922. Mr Levett owned the farm and house behind Justin's Court Lodge.

Neither Mr Leveett nor his helpers were qualified builders, a fact that becomes obvious when viewing inside the house. Floors are not level and walls are not straight, for example.

It is believed that Mr Levett built the house largely of secondhand materials and certainly the oak in the window frames appears to pre-date the house.

The house was built in what was the orchard of Court Lodge, and one of the original trees, a pear tree thought to be more than 100 years old, is still standing in the garden.

After the death of Mr Levett the house was not occupied by his family. It was rented out to an insurance organisation and during the war was requisitioned by the Army and used to house British and Canadian troops.

It was also used to store poison gas and later on became a German prisoner-of-war camp.

After the war the family sought compensation which took until 1955 to be settled. They received £2,000 which was used for renovation prior to its sale in 1956.

Bognor Regis

The Dome House, the Bognor Regis College of Education, now houses students. Once it played host to royalty. It was built in about 1790 by London MP Sir Richard Hotham after he discovered that visiting Bognor was the ideal rest cure.

Sir Richard planned to turn Bognor into another Brighton – and built The Dome in the vain hope that George III would use the place as a seaside residence. Although the king never did arrive, the place was visited by the Prince of Wales, later Regent, and then George IV stayed there in 1796 for two weeks.

From 1807 until 1811 it became the holiday home of the Regent's young daughter, Princess Charlotte, who became a familiar sight in the town and on the beach. The building is of warm brick, with bands of ochre and grey brickwork, and echoes some of the classical forms made fashionable by the Adam brothers in the arches above the central doorway and lower storey windows.

Bolney

Earning a crust in days gone by was no easy matter, as Alfred Worsfold of Bolney would have been pleased to tell you.

As baker for the village, Alfred was out of bed by 4 a.m. and getting the oven to baking heat – on Fridays and Saturdays he worked through the night getting the weekend supply of bread ready.

But if you think Alfred looked on Sunday as a day of rest you would be wrong, for that was the day he did the paperwork.

His wife Eva worked in the shop which is called The Bakery in The Street, Bolney, and is still used for that purpose today.

Alfred was at the bakery from 1933 until 1946 when he was forced to retire for health reasons.

The building was constructed in the days of Queen Victoria by the local squire, who lived at nearby Wykehurst and aimed to supply Bolney and the surrounding rural areas.

In 1892 a fire seriously damaged the building, and it was rebuilt using sandstone to the original specifications.

Boreham Street

White Friars nestles in the village of Boreham Street enjoying peaceful views of surrounding farmland and the rolling Sussex Weald.

It was built by the Benbridge family in 1721, and formed a part of the Ashburnham Estate.

Originally known as Montegue House, this unusual Grade II listed building, with its mellow brickwork and distinctive chimneys, has long provided a landmark for both visitors and villagers.

It was converted into a country house hotel in the Thirties and the proprietors have retained as much of the house's 18th century fabric and character as possible.

But the oldest portion of White Friars is the stone and brick crow-stepped chimney breast on the north-east wall, which dates from the 16th century.

An 18th century farmworker's cottage next to the hotel has been converted to provide eight bedrooms.

White Friars has many interesting architectural features.

The main front of the building faces east, and bears a sundial with the date of 1721, the initials B.I.M. and the arms of the Benbridge family.

The north-east front has a stone Venetian window on the ground floor, with Ionic pilasters. Its doorway has fluted Ionic half-columns and a door of six fielded panels, flanked by side-lights, above which a tile-hung bay has been built out on brick pillars.

Bosham

The site of the present Bosham church was once occupied by the Romans, who built a basilica – an oblong hall used as a court or church – there.

Many pieces of Roman pottery have been found on the floor of Holy Trinity Church and Roman bricks can be seen along the walls.

The Roman occupation of Britain came to an end at the beginning of the sixth century and the basilica, like many others, fell into decay.

The first record of Christianity in Sussex came soon after, with an account by the Venerable Bede (673-735) who wrote of the conversion of the South Saxons.

"But the whole of the kingdom of the South Saxons was ignorant of the name and faith of God. There was, however, a certain monk there by the name of Dicul, who had a very small monastery in a place which is called Boshanhamm, a spot surrounded by woods and sea.

"In it were five or six bretheren who served the Lord in a life of humility and poverty. None, however, of the natives of the country cared either to imitate their life or to listen to their preaching."

So it would seem Christianity was alive, though not exactly flourishing in Bosham, while the rest of Sussex had lapsed into heathenism.

The church itself seems to have been built later, possibly during the rule of King Canute, who succeeded to the throne in 1017. Certainly the tower, nave and chancel are Saxon and probably early 11th century.

It seems the King had a home at Bosham, and requested that his eight-year-old daughter be buried in the church. Yet it wasn't until 1865 that the vicar, the Rev. H. Mitchell, offered concrete evidence.

He had the supposed site of the tomb excavated and a stone coffin was found a few feet below the level of the floor. In it were the remains of a child aged about eight.

Archaeologists confirmed the workmanship on the coffin undoubtedly related to the reign of Canute.

Bosham

The Mill at Bosham has seen its fair share of village history, with – if legends are to be believed – Romans landing, pillaging Danes and King Canute unsuccessfully trying to stop the sea.

Ratham Mill was mentioned in the Domesday Book, and appears on 450-year-old maps. However, the building in its present form appears on drawings dated from the last century.

The existing waterwheels were installed in about 1885, replacing earlier ones, and were last used in about 1924.

The mill is sited in one of the prettiest parts of the village, and currently houses the Bosham Sailing Club on the quay.

Once Bosham Quay saw the arrival of boats carrying coal, corn and oysters. The coal and corn now go by road, and the oyster cargoes no longer come in.

In the ninth century the Danes attempted to loot the village, and legend says they made off with the church bell. As the locals gave chase the Danes threw the tenor bell overboard at Cobnor, since renamed Bell Hole.

It is said that whenever Bosham Bells ring out, the stolen tenor can be heard off Cobnor, chiming with her sister bells and completing the full peal.

Vespian, the Roman commander of the second legion, is reputed to have had a camp and villa at Bosham, and Canute is also supposed to have paddled his feet in the waves there.

There seems little doubt he did live there, but the other legend is less likely to be true. It probably grew up after an unsuccessful attempt by the king to divert the course of the sea using dykes.

Bramber

Bramber is a village overflowing with notable examples of historic architecture. There are the remains of a Norman castle, built soon after 1066 by William de Braose and later stormed and sacked by Parliamentarians in 1641.

There is also St. Mary's, a half timbered building standing on a site granted to the Knights Templars in the 12th century.

Less well known, but of undoubted historical importance, is the Old Priory which stands in The Street.

Its beginnings lie far away from the rarified world of kings and titles, for The Old Priory was built for a simple yeoman, in about 1370.

The building boasts elaborate carvings to the main timber framing, an internal aisle linking the two main halls, and three large inglenook fireplaces.

Bramber was once known as a Rotten Borough, although this label had more to do with the inhabitants than with the buildings. For it meant candidates had been returned to Parliament for the area in less than straightforward circumstances.

Election bribery became such a part of the village, that the villains even had their own pubs where they held court and bought drinks on the eve of an election.

But in 1768, when there were just 34 votes cast, this made all the difference.

If things got really tough, candidates were also not above a straight cash bribe, and one man was reportedly offered £1,000 for his vote.

The man, who lived in a three shillings-a-year rented cottage was either high principled or dim witted for he turned it down . . . or perhaps the other candidate offered more.

Brightling

Follies are fun. Not the multi-million pound high-fliers that bring governments down and put taxes up. But the frolicsome follies that come paid for out of private pockets and a wealth of good old English eccentricity.

Such is Jack Fuller's Sugar Loaf at Brightling. It is one of the best known landmarks in East Sussex and certainly the most super folly.

Jack Fuller was an eighteenth century Brightling squire and, appropriately, he was and is known as Mad Jack Fuller. But mad in the very best of sense. The Sugar Loaf emerged from a bet when he wagered he could see the spire of nearby Dallington Church from his home in Brightling Park.

He couldn't, of course, but that wasn't allowed to stand in the way. He promptly had the conical sandstone 30ft. folly rushed up – looking like and old-time sugar lump and, of course, a church spire – and pointed it out from his study window to the luckless opposition gambler. This was about 1821, history says. And it also says he won his bet.

That wasn't the end of it, naturally, with a chap like Mad Jack. He found he was stuck with a bizarre building with a door, an upstairs room and a cubby-hole atop. So he compounded the whole daft affair.

He dug up two proverbial yokels, offered them the proverbial bag of guineas and asked them to shack up in his ludicrous folly for a year. At the end of that time Jolly Jack was going to the Royal Society (no less) with the claim that he had discovered a pair of dirty but genuine Ancient Britons who had survived the centuries.

It didn't work. Today Jack might be able to cull up scruffy Ancient Briton types at any pop concert. But his yokels were more traditional stuff and threw in the towel after a mere couple of months.

The Sugar Loaf was only one folly anyway within a lifetime of them for Mad Jack. In 1808 he sprung his 22-stone frame upon the Houses of Parliament and claimed it cost him £22,000 in bribes to get there – plus £30,000 subscribed by the county.

Brighton

The original Brighton Aquarium was built in 1872 at a cost of £140,000 – an enormous sum of money for the time.

The whole Aquarium concourse on the seafront was designed by a Mr E. Birch. His elegant stone arches on marble pillars can be seen today, adding a somewhat classical air to the building.

Formerly, the entrance at the western end featured an elaborate archway. But this was removed in 1927 and the only remaining piece of this is the clock tower at the entrance to the Palace Pier.

The Aquarium was rebuilt and refurbished in the late 1920s, and its sumptuous new attractions were opened in a formal and impressive ceremony by Prince George – later King George VI.

One of the features of the new Aquarium was a ballroom, a popular courting place of the Thirties.

Later this became a motor car museum while in 1969 it was rebuilt to house the new Brighton Dolphinarium, now one of the town's most popular tourist attractions.

While excavation was going on, workmen came across part of the original coal harbour, alongside which was sited the old Chain Pier.

Parts of the original sea wall, which protected the town before the building of Madeira Drive, were also uncovered.

Brighton

Patronised by nobility, gentry and the Prince Regent himself, the Chapel Royal, in North Street, was an essential part of fashionable Brighton.

Founded by the Rev Thomas Hudson, the Vicar of Brighton, in 1793, it was intended as a central Chapel of Ease to the town's tiny – and remote – St. Nicholas parish church, which could not cater for the newly-enlarged summer population.

However, there were those who thought the Vicar's motives were an ambitious desire for Royal prestige, influence and financial gain.

Certainly the building enjoyed the patronage of the Prince Regent and his court, and it was situated close to the Royal Pavilion. Prinny laid the foundation stone in 1793, and it opened for worship in 1795, attended by the prince.

By 1800 the Chapel Royal had become Brighton's fashionable place at which to worship. Services were attended by titled summer visitors and often by the Prince Regent and members of the Royal Family. After consecration on August 16, 1803, it became open all year, instead of just the Brighton season of June to September.

In later years the Prince Regent stopped attending and opened his own Royal Chapel in Castle Square in 1822. There is a story that he became displeased by a sermon preached at the Chapel Royal on immorality.

Several members of the Royal Family attended after 1822, including the Duke of York and the Duchess of Gloucester. But the popularity of Brighton and the Chapel declined after the death of George IV, and the last Royal visitor was Princess Augusta who died in 1840.

In 1978, the Chapel Royal parish ceased to exist, and the church returned to its early 19th century status, by being amalgamated with the parish of St. Peter's.

Brighton

Almost as well-known a local landmark as the Royal Pavilion, Hannington's is Brighton's oldest and largest department store.

It was in 1808, when Brighton had fewer than 10,000 inhabitants, that Mr Smith Hannington opened his shop at 2, North Street, to "serve the Quality with silks and satins."

Three years later, the eldest son of King George III became Prince Regent, and his association with Brighton made it a fashionable town and health resort.

Enterprising Mr Hannington brought in all the latest styles from Paris and London to attract the custom of the elegant ladies who surrounded the Prince Regent.

The Prince's mistress, Mrs Fitzherbert, and Lady Downshire, Lady Hertford and Lady Barrymore all purchased their exclusive fashions from Hannington's.

Within Brighton's limited boundary, North Street became the town's main business street. The shop flourished, and in 1814 extended further along North Street. In 1820, the Royal Arms began to appear on the bill-heads, with the words: "Linen and Woollen Draper to His Majesty."

On Smith Hannington's death in 1855, his eldest son Charles took charge. He was said to be a true gentleman, who thought highly of his staff, allowing them a 5½ day week – revolutionary for those days.

The last member of the Hannington family to be associated with the store was Dorothy Hannington, who died in 1966.

The store continued to expand its premises into East Street and around the corner into Market Street, and the present buildings are very much a mixture, although unified by bijou display windows, distinctive pale "pompadour" blue panelling on the exterior, and the familiar Hannington sign above, in gold and silver.

Brighton

The Palace Pier is as synonymous with Brighton as the Prince Regent and sticks of rock. More than two million people visit it each year and it stands as a monument to British engineering.

When the Palace Pier Company was first formed in 1886, the Brighton Chain Pier was still in existence, occupying a site opposite the eastern end of the Aquarium.

As it was one of the conditions enforced by the Board of Trade that as soon as the new pier was completed the Chain Pier was to be renewed, the company took it over for £15,000.

The Chain Pier stood until a ferocious storm swept it away on the night of December 4, 1896 – 73 years after its completion.

The first pile of the Palace Pier was driven in on November 7, 1891, and work progressed until the skeleton of steelwork was completed to a point short of the pier head.

The promoters then fell short of cash, and work stopped for several years, to the annoyance of local residents.

Eventually, the Palace Pier Company was taken over by Sir John Howard, and work began again. In 1899, the pier was opened to the public, complete with the delicate central arches. The same year the first pile was driven in for the pier head.

In 1901, this extension, as well as the famous theatre, were also opened to the public.

During World War One the authorities took charge of the pier as numerous safety precautions were taken, including a look-out!

When the promenade was widened in 1930, the pier entrance was set back about 40ft. and it was then the present canopy and clock tower were erected, the original toll houses being preserved for sentimental reasons.

At the outbreak of World War Two the Army took possession and part of the centre portion was blown up. German dive bombers made several attempts to destroy the pier, but only near misses were recorded.

The pier was re-opened to the public on June 6, 1946.

Brighton

Preston Manor outside Brighton has seen many changes in its lifetime, beginning as a Saxon settlement.

The name Preston is derived from the Anglo-Saxon word Preston, meaning Priest's Holding which indicates a settlement between 900 and 1000 AD.

By the time of the Domesday Book, 1086, the property had the status of a manor and belonged to the Bishopric of Chichester.

Preston became Crown Land in 1559, and was leased to Richard Elrington and his descendants, and 69 years later Thoma Shirley bought the property.

Little is known of the medieval manor of Preston but it is clear it was the property of the Bishops of Chichester.

The two roomed medieval house remained largely unaltered until the latter half of the sixteenth century after which a survey was made by John Norden.

This showed a large triple gabled house surrounded with walled knot gardens. Interestingly, in 1670, the hearth tax returns showed the place had no less than 18 hearths!

Brighton

Once the haunt of Noel Coward and Charles Chaplin, the Royal Crescent Hotel, in Marine Parade, is one of Brighton's best-known seafront hotels.

It stands on the site of a house once owned by George Canning, Britain's Foreign Minister from 1822 and Prime Minister for a few months before his death in 1827.

The story goes that Canning built a passage under the road to the shore and King George IV came for secret meetings with him.

The present hotel was built in 1848 as two large houses and was converted to a hotel ten years later. The 66-room hotel, described by Egon Ronay as a "delightful reminder of a vanished age" became a favourite of Noel Coward and his theatrical set. It became a popular place for actors to stay while playing the Theatre Royal.

Famous visitors have included the late Sir Ralph Richardson and Charlie Chaplin.

One of the hotel's bars is named after Chaplin and the restaurant after Canning.

The hotel is officially classified as being of historic and architectural interest.

Brighton

Edmund Savage, first landlord of the Royal Pavilion Tavern, Brighton, in 1816, had quite a sense of humour.

A successful coal merchant, he turned his talents to the hotel and catering business when he opened the original Royal Pavilion Hotel.

But his ambitions to name one of the bars The Gin Palace fell foul of royalty.

For Mrs Fitzherbert, wife of King George IV, lived next door in the building that is now the YMCA, and she strongly objected to having a Gin Palace so close.

Her fears were probably based on the worry that it would lead to further merciless lampooning from the leading caricaturists of the day, Gilray and Cruickshank.

The two were unaware that the King and Mrs Fitzherbert were legally married. The fact didn't come to light until 1905 when King Edward allowed the security box in Coutts to be opened to reveal the certificate.

So using all her influence, Mrs Fitzherbert managed to stop Mr Savage calling his bar the Gin Palace. Unabashed, he took one look at Mrs Fitzherbert's home towering above and hit on a new name.

"Her house blocks out all the light to my bar, so I shall name it Shades," he announced. From then on the name stuck.

Brighton

After prominent local magistrate, Sir David Scott, bought the Oriental Garden site in Brighton in 1827, he built Sillwood House.

Sir David broke up the garden and on the central portion, which had been reserved for the Athenaeum, he constructed a house for his own residence.

It was named Sillwood House after Sillwood Park, Sunninghill, in Berkshire, the seat of his uncle, Sir Jaxes Sibbald.

He chose Amos Henry Wilds as the architect, having seen his work on Oriental Place and Terrace.

The work started in August 1827 and exactly a year later was completed. The chief feature was a fine hall with staircase winding round it, and extending the whole height of the building.

It also featured a gentleman's room on the ground floor fitted out like a tent, possibly in the Napoleonic/Malmaison style.

But Sir David did not stay long in Sillwood House, in 1831 it was sold by auction and remained in private occupation for about 50 years more.

In about 1880, two years after the death of one of the more important people in the area, it became a hotel.

Sir Francis Goldsmith, who died aged 78 as the result of an accident at Waterloo Station, was responsible for the major development of the Wick Estate.

These included many examples of Hove's finest architecture and possibly the present Maples store in Western Road.

After Sir Francis' death he was succeeded by his nephew, Julian Goldsmid, who died in 1896 leaving eight daughters, but no sons.

The estate therefore passed to Osmund d'Avigdor, and in the same year he was granted authority to take the surname Goldsmid which he added after his previous surname.

Brighton

They don't seem to be a recognisable phenomena today. But if you'd been around Wykeham Terrace in the heart of Brighton during the mid-1880's you'd have seen lots of fallen women.

The terrace was built between 1822 and 1830 as a neat row of Victorian Gothic houses for Brighton's fast expanding gentry belt. But they weren't the only section of the population which was expanding, whichever way you look at it.

Prostitution, too, became rampant with ladies thus engaged freely selling themselves at sites such as the Pavilion Lawns, Church Street, Edward Street and even outside the Theatre Royal, would you believe.

Business, though, obviously had its recessions and to pick up the social bill for it' all St. Mary's Home for Female Penitents was set up in 1855 in building occupying the whole side of Queen Square and most of the houses in Wykeham Terrace.

It must have been a mixed blessing for ladies used to a rougher life. In St. Mary's strictness had a capital S.

Bad language was out and humility and silence was in as the Church, who ran the home, homed in on the immoral lost souls.

Customers there were aplenty though, women that is. In 1859 there were 325 prostitutes recorded in Brighton, with 25 under 16 and a general guess that doubling these figures would have still been an under estimate.

The home for depraved females was founded by the Rev George Wagner and it really swung into its soul saving stride after his death when his son continued the good work.

St. Mary's expanded into a hospital for the poor, a nursery for orphans, an infirmary for OAP's. It even ran coal and provident clubs and a blanket lending society.

Things didn't always proceed smoothly. The home was brought into disrepute in 1863 when a nurse there was accused of murdering her four-year-old step-brother.

History seems to have judged it a frame-up but she was jailed for 20 years before ending her days away in Canada and leaving St. Mary's with a reputation to live down.

Today Wykeham Terrace is the height of respectability again, after suffering the ravages of time and a spell in squatters' hands.

It's been renovated and turned into a prime row of town houses. The only things that fall around here now are leaves in autumn.

Broadbridge Heath

The secret ingredient in the hefty pudding Mrs Ann Whale cooked for her husband James was white mercury. She had cooked a super pud before – brimful with spiders. But they just made it more crunchy.

White mercury, one pennyworth bought from a Horsham chemist, packed more of a punch. Mr Whale was obligingly sick and died the next morning.

It wasn't long before Mrs Whale followed with an even more horrible exit. She was burnt alive at the stake, reputedly being the last woman to die such a death in England.

It all happened in the 1750's at Corsletts Farm, Broadbridge Heath, near Horsham. It was rented by the Whale and Pledge families.

In the time honoured tradition of hate thy neighbour, they did. Especially it was a case of Mr Whale versus Mrs Sarah Pledge. He barred her from his house and read the riot act over relationships.

So Mrs Pledge came in through the back door, so to speak, and suggested to Mrs Whale that they should solve the problem in a final way – with her hubby's death.

What followed is recorded for history in a frank confession the murderesses gave to John Wicker and Samuel Blunt, justices of the peace, on July 6, 1752.

After Mr Whale had eaten the pudding he wasn't immediately affected. He even went to see his landlord for a rent receipt. But the mercury caught up with him and he started to vomit later that evening, dying eventually early next morning.

When the truth came out it was lurid. Mrs Pledge alleged Mrs Whale promised her half a guinea to buy a gown if she would obtain the poison, and £10 to look after her children if she was hanged.

They were, said a commentator of the time "two perfidious, traitorous, malicious, devilish women."

The trial was at Horsham Assizes before Sir John Willes, Lord Chief Justice of the Court of Common Appeal and Sir Thomas Denison and the charge was murder – or petty treason as it was listed then.

The judge made a most sympathetic and humane speech to the court, which records say had everyone moved. And then he said Mrs Whale should die by fire and Mrs Pledge should hang!

The women both received the sacrament on the day before they were executed and they both freely forgave each other.

Buckham Hill

Beeches Farm at Buckham Hill, near Uckfield, is a fine example of an Elizabethan farmhouse.

It boasts exposed beams and an owner of the farmhouse Mrs Vera Thomas found a coin placed there by the builders to date their work.

The gardens are open all year round and the inside of the property can also be viewed by appointment.

The area is bounded by the River Ouse and Ringmer and Horsted Parva, records a contemporary history book on the area. The book, A History of Sussex, by T. W. Horsfield, also notes the population at the time numbered just 581. Other major houses in the area included Isfield Place.

Bucks Green

Right next to the River Arun at Bucks Green is Wanford Mill. The converted mill house is around 400 years old – and the original mill is believed to date from the late 13th century.

Built of brick with part-boarded elevations under a tiled roof, the mill house is listed as a building of architectural and historic interest.

The four-bedroom house, in a picturesque village near Horsham, still retains some of the original internal timbers.

It stands in two acres of land which includes a half-acre mill pond at the front. The owners of Wanford Mill have fishing rights over the Arun.

Burton

The water mill is as evocative of England as cricket on the village green. Once the water mill formed an important part of rural life and where there was a stream the chances were a mill would be located nearby.

Sadly, many have now fallen into disrepair or been pulled down but the Burton Mill, near Petworth, has survived as a reminder of a different age.

The present mill dates back to 1780 when it was occupied by Messrs Linfield and Co., a partnership between John Linfield and John Ibbetson.

When the country feared a French invasion in 1801, the mill announced that if necessary it could produce 14 sacks of flour each weighing 280lbs. every 24 hours.

Various tenant millers occupied the property until the end of the 19th century, by which time cheap grain was coming in from America in ever increasing quantities.

In 1978 the mill was painstakingly restored by Charles Muddle, who comes from an old Sussex milling family, and a team of helpers.

The history of the site goes back much further than 1780, for the mill was built on the site of an ancient iron forge.

Before that there was a much older mill and fishery in the area.

Burwash

The lovely Jacobean house of Bateman's, south of Burwash, is chiefly associated with author Rudyard Kipling, who lived there for 34 years.

He bought the house, (built in 1634 of local sandstone) in 1902, having made his home in India, America, London, and Rottingdean, where his Burne-Jones relations lived.

Burwash was chosen after Rottingdean had proved too close to Brighton and its sight-seeing trippers. Kipling wanted peace and quiet for his writing.

Although he had written his major Indian works before he came to Sussex, his new material lay in the history and life of the Sussex and Kent countryside.

It was at Bateman's that Kipling completed such books as Puck of Pook's Hill (1906) – the hill itself is visible from the lawn at Bateman's looking west.

Kipling and his wife improved the house considerably, and as early as 1902 had installed their own electricity.

When Kipling died in 1936, Bateman's was bequeathed to the National Trust.

Its walls shelter a wealth of Kipling articles, while the countryside around is intimately described in Puck of Pook's Hill and Rewards and Fairies.

Burwash

One of the most beautiful of Sussex villages, Burwash, was the home of author Rudyard Kipling for more than 30 years until his death in 1936. But in the 18th and 19th century it was famous as a smugglers' centre.

The village abounds in historic buildings. Until about 1700, it was one of the most flourishing centres of the Sussex iron industry, which helps account for the wealth of charming houses and cottages lining the streets.

Chime Cottage, in Church Street, is thought to date from around 1720, but has undergone many conversions since then – the most recent being in 1960.

The most dramatic changes took place 50 years ago, when its old straw thatch was replaced by Norfolk reed.

During the 18th and early 19th centuries the village was notorious for its gangs of smugglers and sheep-stealers. Between 1820 and 1840 Burwash was so full of them it was declared unsafe to travel through.

The history of Burwash, however, can be traced back to the earliest times. its very name derives from the Anglo-Saxon: Burgh or berh was the word for hill and woesse meant bog or marshland. Accordingly, Burwash stands on a hill surrounded by clay soil which is marshland for some of the year.

Chailey

The red brick manor house, Ades at Chailey, has seen many changes since it was built in the early 1700s.

In this century alone it has been a private house, a remand home and a canteen for the Canadian Army!

The original medieval manor was destroyed by fire and nobody is sure whether the present house stands on the site of the original.

The manor, which is now divided into three separate houses, started life at the centre of an estate. The farm it once owned is now quite independent and the grounds are considerably smaller.

Among its owners were the Goring family, famous in Sussex, who lived there at the beginning of the 18th century.

Then came Dr William Russell, better known as Dr Brighton, the man who founded the town as a seaside resort.

"We know he owned the house," said Mr Midgley, "but whether he actually lived here is again uncertain."

Richard Bourchier, who spent 40 years in the East Indies, eight of them as governor of Bombay, owned the house for a while before it was bought by Admiral Markham, M.P.

At some time during the early years of the 19th century the house was occupied by Gen Frederick St. John, second son of the second Viscount Bolingbroke.

When Admiral Markham died the estate was put up for auction in 1837. The sale included Rowheath, Furze Grove, Cinder Farm, Birches, the Frick and the land at Markstakes. The total area was 393 acres.

It included copyholds of the manors of Allington, Balneath and Warningore which shows how interlocked the manors were in those days.

The Ingrams bought Ades and the estate remained more or less intact until it was broken up nearly 100 years later.

Chailey

Lying at the very centre of Sussex, the Chailey Heritage white smock mill dates from 1830, although it was extensively rebuilt a century later after a devastating gale.

Since 1933 the mill has been cared for by Chailey Heritage, the school for handicapped children. It is now used as a Scout headquarters.

However, it has not always held its present geographical position. It began its life as Hammingden Mill in Highbrook, an attractive High Weald hamlet 5½ miles to the north.

In 1844 Mr Bollen of Newhaven needed a replacement for his own mill, which had burned down. He bought the Hammingden Mill and brought it 19 miles to a site overlooking the sea above western Newhaven.

It proved useful as Newhaven smock mill but, by 1864, had gained new owners, who had just built a steam mill at a harbour site near the famed "Tipper" brewery.

However, a Mr Beard, of Chailey, who owned an old post mill, required a replacement.

Hearing of the redundant state of Newhaven's smock mill, he had it moved up to Chailey where it has stayed for the last 122 years.

The mill, now enjoying a well-deserved retirement, was rebuilt in 1933 after it was decapitated by a gale. Several years later a similar accident occurred and the mill was restored to the state it is in today.

It was last worked in around 1911 when it had three pairs of underdrift stones driven by an auxiliary engine via an external pulley. The white smock tower had three floors held securely to the single-storey brick base by stout external tie rods.

Chichester

The Church of All Saints in the Pallant at Chichester was built during the 13th century, and is the only one to be mentioned in the Domesday Book.

The lancet windows are typical of the period, but those in the east wall of the chancel were restored in 1842.

Ian Nairn and Nikolaus Pevsner, in their book Sussex, rather unkindly describe the building as "simple as a barn".

The poet and biographer William Hayley was baptised in the church in 1745. Among the eminent Cicestrians buried in the church are members of the Gruggen and Comper families who were partners in the Old Chichester Bank.

The word Pallant is derived from the Latin palantia, meaning exclusive jurisdiction, and it was the Archbishop of Canterbury who had exclusive palatine rights over 12 acres of Chichester until 1552.

The church itself became redundant in 1970.

Chichester

St. Richard, Bishop of Chichester (1245-54), enabled a vicarage house to be built at Cuckfield and endowed it with land.

The present Old Vicarage is a Grade II listed house. Its grounds are dominated by a large ornamental pond, which is mentioned in the Domesday Book.

It is believed to have been stocked with carp by monks in the 11th century.

Church records indicate the Rev Charles Ashburnham began building the vicarage house in 1780, and it was finished in September 1781.

The Rev Henry Plimley, vicar in 1818, borrowed £700 from Queen Anne's Bounty to enlarge the house and build a sitting room with a bow window.

A later vicar, the Rev T. A. Maberley, had a loan from the same source to build a bow window to the dining room, add a drawing room, a room above the drawing room, and kitchen offices.

The last vicar to occupy the house was the Rev C. W. G. Wilson, and it was sold in 1937 to Col A. H. Bell.

Col Bell died in 1968 at the age of 89 and Mrs Bell died in 1971. They were noted for their support of Cuckfield activities – particularly the parish tea party on Trinity Sunday.

This has continued to be held at the house with the permission of subsequent owners.

Chichester

Pallant House, described as the finest building in historic Chichester, has just been restored to its former glory.

The Queen Anne mansion had been left in a sorry state after its use as council offices. But now, after a £150,000 facelift, the house has been carefully restored and opened to the public as one of the south's leading art galleries.

Pallant House was built in 1713 by wealthy wine merchant Henry Peckham, a grandson of Sir Henry Peckham, who was Chichester's MP in 1647.

Peckham was still under 30 when he had amassed a fortune large enough to build the house using the finest craftsmen of the day.

But although he closely followed the style of the period he adopted one bizarre touch. He hired a sculptor to make stone figures of two ostriches to stand at the entrance of the house in the Pallant.

The bird featured in the crest adopted by Peckham's family.

But, as the house's official history relates: "The sculptor who undertook the making of these birds had clearly never seen an ostrich and had to rely on second hand descriptions."

The statues have earned the house its familiar nick-name of "the Dodo house."

Chichester

Things nautical have always played an important part in the life of The Ship Hotel, Chichester.

This fine Georgian building was built in 1790 as a private house for Admiral Sir George Murray. The admiral commanded a squadron with Nelson at the Battle of Copenhagen in 1801.

Many of the 30 bedrooms at The Ship are named after clipper ships or famous vessels which fought at Trafalgar.

On April 21, 1944, a little before D-Day, General Eisenhower dined at the hotel with senior officers of Royal Air Force Fighter Command.

The list of those who attended and a menu of the dinner is now framed in the reception hall.

The Ship has an Adam staircase and a colonnade leading from the main entrance. The hotel is next to Priory Park, where the remains of Chichester Castle can be seen.

Chichester

It was the sight of Vicars' Close in the precincts of Chichester Cathedral that gave John Keats the inspiration for some of the greatest imagery of his poem, the Eve of St. Agnes.

Keats, one of the major romantic poets of the 19th century, visited Sussex in 1819 and began to write the poem at his lodgings in Eastgate House, Chichester.

Initially, the Close, a long, narrow lane of 15th century houses, was an enclosure in which lived the Vicars' Choral, who ate in the beautiful refectory, the Vicar's Hall (now a restaurant) at the North End.

Regrettably, however, in 1825, a wall of partition was built down the centre of the Close, the gatehouse which closed the southern side was removed in 1831, and the frontages of the houses on the eastern side were turned round to form shops in South Street.

The north end of Vicars' Close contains the Hall, with its fine timber roof, and a 14th century lavabo in the north wall. Situated below is a late 12th century vaulted undercroft, of simple but impressive proportions.

The 15th century houses were modernised in the 18th century and are today private houses.

The pathway, flanked by attractive gardens, leads to a narrow passage, which in turn leads to the cloisters.

Chiddingly

Colour prejudice was petal, rather than skin, deep in the Middle Ages. And it is reputed to have had an unfortunate effect on a luckless knight who went a'courting at Chiddingly. His trouble was to wear the wrong coloured rose, which in turn placed him on the wrong side of his loved one during The War of the Roses.

He was pragmatic in his approach though. He is said to have swapped roses at the drop of a visor on initial rejection. But it didn't do a jot of good.

So when his love climbed into the four poster with the wrong chap at a romantically named house called Pekes, the knight clanked for a final lament underneath her bedroom window. And that sad memorial act is what he is supposed to have done every year since on the anniversary.

The house's history has been traced back to Tudor origin, when it was built to replace a Norman hall.

That's where the name comes from. The Normans didn't take long to reach Chiddingly when they came ashore at Pevensey, and when they did the Conqueror called on one Mr de Peke to accept ownership of the manor. He didn't hesitate!

Years later he was followed by a well chronicled family, the Jefferays, who produced the notorious hanging judge.

They were seated in Sussex early in the fifteenth century and were responsible for many alterations and extensions to Pekes.

We probably have them to thank for the remarkable mural and paintings at the house. They are unusual chiefly because they are only thought to have seen 60 years exposure before being covered up around 1630 by later wall panelling.

It is thought the paintings were the work of a travelling artist, and another remarkable thing about them is that they were probably an artistic stop-gap to patch up irregular wall surfaces.

The method used was to drape coarse linen from floor to roof, apply a thin coat of plaster and then suitable flower murals and the like.

Crawley

A 15th century Crawley building stands as a monument to Alphonse Karr's maxim – the more things change, the more they stay the same.

For the building has been used as a farm, a cafe and now a bank, while still managing to look like a chocolate box timbered cottage.

The National Westminster bank in Crawley High Street started life as a building called Mitchells. It is of typical Tudor design with a central hallway rising to the full height of the house.

It was then known as Black Dog Farm, and later still The Olde Punch Bowle Cafe.

Both wings of the house have projecting first floors, though the south side has been built under with 18th century brickwork.

The building would probably have had a simple hole in the roof to act as a chimney, but soon after its construction, a proper chimney was added.

This meant two doors were lost; one behind the fireplace, and another which today can be seen as an arched lintel on the outside. It was replaced by a smaller door which has been removed to form the second of the projecting long windows to the bank office.

Cuckfield

The earliest records of the Manor of Cuckfield date back to the Norman Conquest, and the house and grounds are steeped in legend.

One surrounds the great tree which stood next to the delightful brick 16th century gatehouse. It was known as the Doom Tree, and the shedding of a branch was always taken as a foreboding sign of the imminent death of the male heir.

Nearer the present, Anne Sergison, who lived at Cuckfield Park until 1846 and died aged 85, was known as the Wicked Dame Sergison because of her reputedly vile and vindictive temper.

The Sergison family refused to allow the London to Brighton railway to pass through the village in 1841, which is why many commuters in Cuckfield must go to Haywards Heath to travel to London.

It is said that Dame Sergison's ghost used to swing on the gates at the park entrance, until it was exorcised by three clergymen.

Cuckfield Manor and grounds were originally among lands conferred as a reward to the Earl of Warenne, Lord of the Rape of Lewes, who had fought with the Conqueror at the Battle of Hastings.

In 1573, the Earl of Derby sold his portion of the manor to Henry Bowyer, a wealthy and successful ironmaster of the Sussex Weald. It was he who ordered the construction in 1574 of the present building, which took several years to complete.

The house is approached by a pleasing brick gatehouse of the later 16th century, which has four angle turrets lighted by bullseyes and round-headed loops.

The Sergison family, who owned the house from 1693, used to bury their dead at night, and the coffin was traditionally passed beneath the archway of the gatehouse the day and night before interment.

Cuckfield

Marshalls in Cuckfield provided the setting for one of the most extraordinary events Sussex has ever seen.

Known as the Sleeping Maid of Cuckfield it started on September 15, in 1807, when the housemaid fell asleep in her attic bedroom in the house. Nothing unusual about that – except that the girl slept non-stop for an astonishing eight days.

No-one could wake her and when the worried employers, Mr and Mrs Wood, called the village doctor he diagnosed her body temperature had also dropped. But apart from that he could find no explanation for what was happening. Nor indeed could the girl when she awoke on September 22.

Happily, she suffered no ill effects from her experience, although the tale subsequently became something of a local legend in the county.

The house itself was originally timber framed and erected in about 1575, with the chimneys at each end probably dating from the Jacobean period. It was also re-fronted in the 18th century, although unlike most modern additions, this work has added rather than detracted from the property as a whole.

In Victorian times an additional wing was built, although in the 1950's this was pulled down to reveal Tudor brick panelling between structural timbers which had been hidden from view for 100 years. The Grade Two listed building was one of the Minor Manors of Cuckfield and is mentioned in the Chichester Records Office Court Manorial Rolls.

Cuckfield

You couldn't accuse Timothy Burrell of breaking any social contract when it came to employing William Gates as a footman at Ockenden Manor, Cuckfield, back in the 1600's.

His records reveal with stark financial clarity that he handed over 50s. as his yearly wages and the more princely sum of £4 to his coachman to maintain a discreet differential.

They were both doubtless grateful. But then living in the splendour of Ockenden Manor must have had other compensations.

The Burrells are one of the oldest of Sussex families. The Cuckfield burial register reports that in September 1608 the manor was burnt and then bought by a William Burrell from the Michel family.

So started an occupancy that lasted for centuries, with the house being rebuilt by William, and his wife Frances proudly placing their initials up front on the finished product.

The family, who trace their links back to Radulphus Burrell of circa 1270, went on to become leading iron masters of the county and vicars of Cuckfield too.

The Rev Gerard Burrell held the position in 1483 and was the archdeacon of Chichester Cathedral.

Returns of the Hearth Tax of 1665 show four Burrell families living at Cuckfield – and 14 hearths at Ockenden.

But it is diarist and barrister Timothy Burrell who captures inflation-reeling imaginations. He lived from 1683 to 1714 and these are just some of his expenses he notched up at the manor:

- Fourteen shillings spent on a day out at Lewes.
- A total of £22 17s. spent on a day out at London.
- Five quarts of brandy – 5s.
- For the keep of two calves – 6d. a week.
- Six bushels of wheat at 17s. 4d.
- A gift to the poor of £1 5s.
- Claret at 1s. 6d.
- John Holford got £3 for two years wages and £2 for excusing his livery that year!
- 1s. for bleeding by the apothecary!

Ditchling

Cotterlings in Ditchling, with its distinctive tiles, forms an attractive part of one of the historic villages of Sussex. It is rumoured the house was once occupied only by single ladies of the village.

But there was nothing untoward going on behind the doors of the 17th century house . . . for the Turner family, while living at Oldland House, provided Cotterlings for the unmarried daughters of the family.

The two-storey house, with its own two acres of grounds has been owned by the Turner family for generations. The mathematical tiles were a fairly common Sussex feature, and were designed to make a house look as though it was constructed from brick instead of timber.

Ditchling

Sir Frank Brangwyn decided to settle permanently in Ditchling after stopping off at Brighton to take in a silent film version of the Hunchback of Notre Dame.

The world-famous artist had originally set out with a companion for a convalescent motor trip through the South of France. But they never went further than the South of England and a film which, for unrecorded reasons, was the last Sir Frank was ever to see.

He had first come to Ditchling years earlier to recover from a serious operation. So impressed were he and his wife that they bought a house and lived between there and studios he still maintained in Hammersmith.

But London had become crowded and suffocating for the artist. He found increasing peace in a South Downs home. And after his wife's death, and the Hunchback, he lived permanently at Ditchling until his own death there in 1956.

Sir Frank was probably the most famous of the artist community which still flourishes at Ditchling. But he was born far away from the peaceful Sussex retreat where some of his greatest works were completed.

He came into the world on May 12, 1867, at Rue de Vieux Bourg, Bruges, in Belgium. It was a town which was later to honour his memory with a Brangwyn Museum and to suggest that despite his Welsh stock he may have been a Belgian because his name in Flemish translated into Brandy!

Sir Frank's father was an architect who moved to Belgium to work on reproduction ecclesiastical work. He lived there for eight years before returning to an art education in England, an apprenticeship to thinker and artist William Morris and the eventual separation of his parents.

His art progressed by way of water colours, oils and murals until his success far transcended anything his father had expected when he first took him to art school.

One of the most notable works he finished at Ditchling was the Ascent of Man Murals for New York. And his most notable companion during the commission of them was a parrot.

Duncton

The pub sign of the 15th century Cricketers Arms in Duncton, near Petworth, immortalises one of the village's most famous sons – James Dean.

That's not the Rebel Without a Cause actor of the fifties, but the sporting James Dean, one of the giants of 19th century Sussex County Cricket Club history.

Dean was a great friend of his fellow England XI cricketer, the diminutive John Wisden, later to become famous for producing the first editions of that cricketing bible, Wisden's Almanack.

Wisden took over the Swan pub in 1867 and changed its name to the Cricketers. He allowed his chum James to be his tenant for as long as he wished.

James, also known as "Joyous Jemmy", "Dean Swift" and "The Sussex Ploughboy", was born in Duncton in 1816 and dominated Sussex cricket for 25 years from 1835 to 1860. He was still playing at the age of 65.

A sawyer by trade, he worked on the ground staff of Lords for 25 years, and in 1852, started the famous England XI with John Wisden.

In later life, Dean tenanted the Cricketers Arms Inn, and the sign outside the public house still bears his portrait.

Inside, evidence abounds of James Dean's connection with the inn. An illuminated scroll hanging on the bar testifies to his reputation.

Dean had been suffering from asthma and bronchitis for some time, when, on Christmas Eve, 1881, he gathered around his hearth a number of friends, amongst whom was, as always, his long-standing companion, John Wisden.

When the guests rose on Christmas morning they found Dean had died peacefully in his sleep. He was buried in the Old Churchyard in Duncton, not far from the Cricketers Arms.

Easebourne

Dame Alice Hill wasn't a woman to take things lightly.

She lived at Easebourne in the shadow of Cowdray Park. Female outspokenness was not exactly a hallmark of her times, which coincided with Henry VIII's Dissolution of the Monasteries.

When Henry and his supporters tightened their regal strings around the Church it meant the end of Easebourne's famous Augustinian priory and the end of their spell in secluded Sussex for the nuns and their prioress.

That proved too much for Dame Alice, a sub-prioress. Legend has it that she placed a curse on the house and male owners of Cowdray's monastery grounds.

It didn't work – at least not immediately. It was not until 1793 that the stately Cowdray home was gutted by fire. By then the priory at Easebourne was but a memory and the building used, as it is today, as a house.

But its heyday had seen different times. Founded in 1248 by Sir Frank de Bohun, the priory was endowed with Easebourne Church and the chapel-of-ease at Midhurst. Its value at the time was put at £26.

According to records in 1441 the Bishop of Chichester had to dress down the prioress of the day. Her sin was extravagance – and it took the form of numerous lap-dogs, pet monkeys and other less than lordly trappings.

The indulgences came to an abrupt halt!

Side by side, both historically and physically, with the priory is Easebourne church. It has a wall belonging to four parishes – Easebourne, Midhurst, Fernhurst and Lodsworth.

Early parish registers show how the village has changed over the years, from Estbourne, to Esbourne and right through to Easebourne.

But all names probably originate from Essebourne and the tiny Esse tributary which, historical comings and goings apart, continues to flow through the village.

Eastbourne

The Church of St. Saviour and St. Peter, Eastbourne, started life as two separate buildings.

St. Saviour's Church was the first to be built, with the foundation stone laid in 1865. The sister church, St. Peter's, followed 13 years later on a temporary site in Saffrons Road.

But in 1971 the two churches were unified as the Church of St. Saviour and St. Peter, and the old St. Peter's church was demolished.

The original St. Saviour's Church must rank as one of the most unusual gifts ever. It was built by London businessman Mr George Whelper and given to his son who became the first vicar.

The church was built on land given by the 7th Duke of Devonshire, and the church was the fruit of the Tractarian movement which began life in Oxford in the 1830s.

The present church is noted for its broad nave and slender aisles which direct attention to the sanctuary and the altar.

There is also a fresco painting over the chancel arch, showing the church triumphant and Christ glorified.

The converging spaces on either side have three tiers of figures, angels above, the 12 apostles with their symbols in the middle, and martyrs and worshippers below.

The painting is the work of Clayton and Bell, best known for their stained glass. They also designed the glass in the arcades of the sanctuary.

The baptistry and west porches were built in 1898 and the mosaics were the work of Powell of Whitefriars.

A later addition is the chapel of the Blessed Sacrament, and was dedicated on All Saint's Day, 1903. Originally decorated in colour, the design was simplified in 1971.

The altar is of carved oak, and the work of George Jack, who worked for George Street, the architect who designed the church.

There is also a memorial brass of the first vicar in the arched recess between the chapel and the nave.

Eastbourne

The Lambe Inn at Eastbourne is probably one of the oldest pubs in the country, with its cellars and halftimber work dating from the late 12th century.

During the 14th and 15th century, the inn was popularly believed to be a centre for smuggling purposes. Underground passages between the Lambe and a nearby parsonage and cottage testify to this theory.

It was during the course of repairs in 1912 that the inn's ancient half-timber work was discovered. By coincidence, its close neighbour, The Star at Alfriston, was undergoing similar repairs.

Both inns were probably resting places for mendicant friars and pilgrims, travelling to Canterbury or to and from the shrine of Richard De La Wynche at Chichester. Later on, in the 18th century, The Lambe saw the arrival and departure of the London coach.

It is known that officers of the Sussex Regiment held a ball at the Lamb Inn just before they set off for the Battle of Waterloo. When they arrived, the battle was over – and the regiment returned to hold another ball at the Lambe for they had not fired a single shot.

Eastbourne

The Old Parsonage to the north of the Parish Church of St. Mary in Eastbourne dates from the 16th century.

That makes it a mere babe in arms compared with the church itself, which is thought to date from the 12th century.

But, even so, the rubble and flint walls of the Old Parsonage have stood since about 1519 and the building was once the Rectory Manor House and part of Rectory Manor.

Once owned by the Duke of Devonshire, the building stands as a good example of Tudor domestic architecture with its 3ft thick walls.

Externally it is 76ft by 26ft and inside it follows the usual design of a late medieval manor house with a great hall and 10ft wide stone fireplace. At each end of the building there are chambers and cellars underneath.

It formed part of the buildings of the original Manor of Burne and was used as the manorial court house. That function was vital to the manorial system, and it served as a place to maintain and keep records.

In 1791 the Ecclesiastical Commission acquired the property and it was later sold to the Duke of Devonshire. In 1924, the Duke gave the building to the church authorities on condition it should be used for parochial matters.

East Grinstead

Cromwell House and Porch House, in East Grinstead, are adjoining properties, both built during the 16th century. Porch House is the older of the two, and was constructed in the early part of the 16th century.

The remaining original features front on to the street at the west end of the building, and this is complemented by a noteworthy 17th century addition to the rear. It also has a carved stone porch, and a 16th century stone frontage on the east wall.

Cromwell House was built in 1599, and was formerly the Great House, standing three stories high. It was built originally for the powerful Payne family, but in 1928 the east end was badly damaged by fire and afterwards restored by Walter Godfrey of Lewes.

East Grinstead

One of the more attractive country houses in north Sussex is Gullege Farm, on the outskirts of East Grinstead.

It is a timber framed property with a three-gabled Jacobean front which replaced the earlier exterior in 1609. The east and west ends are timber framed with plaster fronting and partly covered with tiles.

A feature are the three chimneys dating from Tudor times. They run the length of the house and the central one boasts an unusual star shape.

The central stack indicates the house was once T-shaped, possibly with a hall reaching to the full height of the house and having a gallery over the fireplace reached by spiral staircases.

Records show a Allfrey of Gullege lived in the area in 1365 and there is also evidence that a settlement existed on the site in Roman and Saxon times.

When the present owners restored the property they found a wall painting dating from 1550. The house also possesses wide oak floorboards, and ironwork on the back door which may have been executed by ironmasters who once lived there.

Local legend suggests that a house at the bottom of the drive leading to Gullege was once lived in by Anne Boelyn and Henry VIII used to meet her there when he was staying at Hever Castle.

It is said that Henry VIII planted the giant oak that stands at the front, but along with the Anne Boleyn legend, that too seems unlikely.

East Grinstead

How do you fancy Standen as a prime example of an "anti-Victorian" house?

Most of us would have no trouble at all in feeling very pro about this elegant building which has now been opened on our behalf by the National Trust two miles south west of East Grinstead.

But when famous architect Philip Webb designed it in the 1890's it came off the drawing board as an artistic protest against that era's prevaling styles and trends.

Webb was a friend and collaborator of famous Victorian reformer of decorative arts, William Morris, which explains the radical thought behind Standen. And even though the years have blurred the breakaway points of design, it's still more than a distinctive property.

The house was begun in 1892 and finished in 1894 for a wealthy solicitor, James Beale, who had a practice in London and whose wife Margaret came from a Birmingham family which claimed links going back to Oliver Cromwell.

A fine pair of cultivated, wealthy high Victorians they must have been. They had a huge house in London, were friends with all the top people of the day and had Standen built as a country hideaway for weekends and eventually retirement.

They couldn't have found anywhere much nicer within reach of the city. It was a site which then was made up of three small farms with views across the Medway Valley to Ashdown Forest.

Then came the not so easy stage of design and getting Mr Webb, with his more than strong portfolio of ideas, to compromise with Mrs Beale and her equally strong collection of more traditional tastes.

Eventually agreement was reached and the house was built with stone from the hillside behind the house, Horsham brick, all finished off with tile hanging and weather board.

Inside, Standen reflects the supreme and cosy confidence of the Victorians. Musical parties and family teas were held in the hall. White Chinese porcelain bought by the Beales in Venice in 1898 decorated the dining room and Morris legendary wallpaper abounded throughout.

The morning room was for Standen's ladies who organised the social events and whirls of the times, and the drawing room still boasts a Morris designed carpet hand knotted at his Merton Abbey workshops.

But all things must pass and so did Standen's founding family. James Beale died in 1912 and his widow continued to live there until her death in 1936.

Etchingham

The history of Haremere Hall, Etchingham, dates from the late 12th century, when the name of Miles de Haremere, Lord of the Manor, is recorded.

But most of the present building, standing on the original site on rising ground above the River Rother, was built in Jacobean style, with a symmetrical stone facade, around 1616.

During and after the English Civil War, the hall was always associated with the Royalist cause. In 1612 it became the property of John Busbridge, whose son, another John, inherited it.

The story goes that the younger John was sleeping in a bedroom overlooking the drive and was awakened by the sound of horses – Cromwell's soldiers advancing.

They took the house, and John was shot and killed. The room in which he slept was, for a long time, left to wind and weather, and much of the furniture in the house was stolen or burnt.

Another version of the story paints him as somewhat of a dandy, for it is said he was spotted by the soliders while posing in a window in a new white-plumed hat.

Sir George Strode, a Royalist wounded at Edgehill, lived at Haremere until he died in 1663. He went abroad when the Royalist cause collapsed, and returned to recover his estates by paying the large fine of £2,850. His descendents succeeded him as Lord of the Manor during the 18th century.

A later owner of the Manor was Sir John Lade, the Master of the King's Horses to the Prince Regent, who was a frequent visitor.

The Hall, situated in 140 acres of rolling parkland, eventually became the property of Lord Killearn, who died in 1964. Jacqueline, Lady Killearn, still owns the house.

The oldest part of the house is a single wall left when fire demolished the building. In the west wing are two small stained-glass windows, in a corridor leading to the kitchens, which bear dates of 1509 and 1603.

Much of the house is panelled in oak, probably dating from the 17th or 18th century.

One interesting feature over the fireplace in the dining room is a Jacobean overmantel, carved with biblical scenes.

Firle

Those in need of a stiff drink after appearing before magistrates at Firle, near Lewes, didn't have to travel far.

For the Ram Inn was once the local court as well as the local pub. People were called into the court room from the bar.

The inn also boasts a 140-year-old till designed for the sovereign and half sovereign.

The building has been used as an inn for more than 300 years, yet during that time just three families have held the licence.

The Mocketts, who retained it for three generations, were followed by the Steadman family, who kept it for just one generation.

The Haffendens took over in 1908 when Stephen Haffenden moved from the Barley Mow.

Fontwell

The Clock House, at Fontwell, was the original stable block to a large 19th century house. It stands in the garden of what is known as Denmans, which also includes an original flint and brick bothy, or garden boy's house, in the same estate.

Both structures date from about 1820, although the tower at the Clock House is of brick and dates from around 1900. The site stands about 65ft above sea level, and a tower was once used as a means of irrigating the old vegetable garden. Water was pumped from a now disused well, up into the tower and then circulated to the garden.

Forest Row

Sir James Richards wasn't known as a timid man.

But one thing which scared him out of his armour was the possibility of a knock on the door of his Brambletye House home at Forest Row.

He did not wait till the rivets fell out of his armour though. One day in 1683 he simply hightailed it from Sussex, fled England and sailed to Spain, never to return.

It was not a forerunner of the VAT man, or even an early insurance collector asking about overdue premiums that made him do a Costa bunk, but the High Sheriff and his men asking nasty questions about alleged treason.

Plainly Sir James did not have any suitable answers with which to placate and parry them, hence his emergency exit.

But the colourful flight, be it fancy legend or truth, was an equally final chapter for the house. It proceeded to fall into ruins!

The loss to history was perhaps greater than the loss of one errant knight. Brambletye House was recorded at Forest Row in the Domesday survey compiled by the Normans in 1086 and the site has a history which can be traced right back to Saxon times.

The Aldham family were lords of the manor during the 14th century and after that it was the Comptons who ruled the roost.

In 1631, Sir Henry Compton, MP for East Grinstead, cemented his position in society by having the present house built. A fine property it was, too, with stout walls of local stone and an architect's design that unusually had it facing north, with five towers linked together by two storeys and a large vaulted basement.

Next to come along was Sir James himself, until that fateful day when he was out hunting and heard news of the treason probe.

Now all that's left of Brambletye House, today part of private property, are three front towers, a ruined basement and the most poignant of memories.

Forest Row

The attractive, stone-built offices of auctioners Powell and Partners are among the oldest buildings in the village of Forest Row.

A detached, timber-framed building, with a slated roof and distinctive porch, the building dates back some 600 years and was originally used as a farm house.

But it has undergone several changes of use over the years. For some years it was used as residential cottages, and later as an antiques shop.

In the 1930s there was a major conversion and the building became the Blue Lantern tearooms.

During the Second World War, the building was taken over by the British American Union and used as an officers' club.

After the war, the building was put up for sale, and purchased by Powell and Partners, a firm of auctioneers, estate agents, surveyors and valuers, who owned other offices in the village at that time.

Forest Row

Michael Hall School in Kidbrooke Park, Forest Row, began life in 1773 as a mansion house built by William Neville, the 42nd Lord Abergavenny.

It was constructed of local iron-stained sandstone from quarries at West Hoathly, in the heart of Ashdown Forest. The mansion was a central block of five bays on four floors, with a pediment to the east over the door, emblazoned with the Abergavenny coat of arms.

The house was occupied by the Abergavenny family until the late 18th century, but in 1802 Kidbrooke Mansion was bought by Charles Abbot MP for £15,375.

Abbot set about improving the parkland and the house, and engaged the famous landscape artist Humphrey Repton, to redesign the park.

Abbot became the first Baron Colchester. He began discussions with Lord Elgin about buying the famous Parthenon marbles for Britain and he also established a village school.

After his grandson, Reginald Charles, became the third Lord Colchester in 1867, the estate was sold in the 1870s to Henry Ray Freshfield, the senior partner in the firm of solicitors to the Bank of England.

During their years at Kidbrooke, the Freshfield family made minor alterations to the estate, including a formal garden with a fountain on the south lawn.

In 1916 the estate was purchased by Sir James Horlick, of malted milk drink fame, and after his death in 1921 by the Hambro family, who used Kidbrooke for weekend visits and holidays.

One of the proudest moments in Kidbrooke history was in 1929, when it hosted a splendid pageant.

This was attended by the Duchess of York (later the Queen Mother), Rudyard Kipling, Vita Sackville-West and A. A. Milne.

In 1945 the building was bought by Michael Hall, a Rudolph Steiner School.

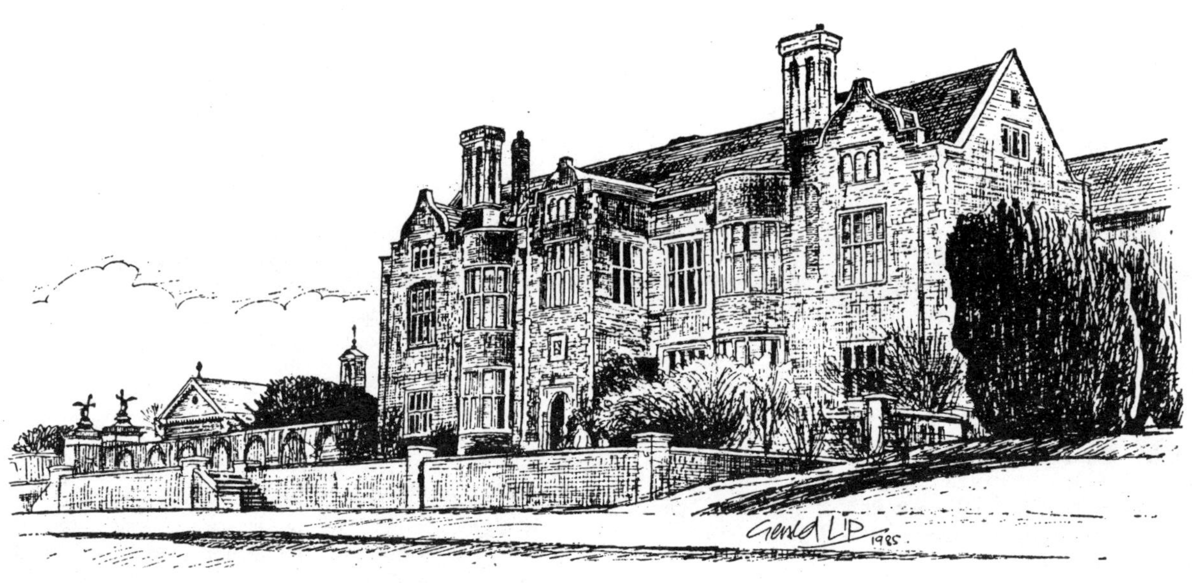

Glynde Place

Lovely Glynde Place, near Lewes, the home of Lord and Lady Hampden and their three children, has a distinguished history going back to the 16th century.

The estate has always been owned by just one family, but it has not always been passed on to a male heir and during the last 800 years there have been four different family names – Waleys, Morleys, Trevors and Brands.

It was the Morleys who built Glynde Place in 1579. It was conceived as a square, with its four sides surrounding a courtyard, which is now a flower garden.

The most famous of the Morleys was Col Herbert Morley, a distinguished soldier and politician. He was MP for Lewes in 1640, and was immediately to become one of the leading soldiers campaigning on behalf of Parliament in Sussex during the Civil War. Eventually he had to buy his pardon from King Charles II.

The Brands inherited Glynde Place during the 18th century and it was during the next century that Henry Brand, former Speaker in the House of Commons, was created Viscount Hampden – a title also used by his Trevor forebears.

Part of the house and grounds are open to the public. The garden is largely made up of lawns and shrubs dominated by a long beech walk put in by the Bishop of Durham.

Goodwood

You could call Carne's Seat, on the Duke of Richmond's estate at Goodwood, a pioneer eating house in the most literal sense.

But there's never been a hamburger near there. This, in its heyday, was a "take two grouse, five pheasants and a dozen oysters" eatery.

The property – which is not open to the public – is a beautiful stone temple built for the second duke in 1743 and thought to have been designed by Roger Morris. In fact, it mostly served as a gastronomic temple by virtue of being used on most occasions as a banqueting house.

The name is thought to have been that of an old servant and friend of Louise de Queroualle, who is said to have lived in a cottage there. And who was she?

Stand by for a slice of Goodwood history. She was the Duchess of Portsmouth, mother of the first duke by King Charles II, having met the king as a lady in waiting to his sister Henrietta, Duchess of Orleans, when she visited the English court. We are told the king and Louise maintained a close relationship until his death and that she was first of his favourites.

When the second duke came along he inherited the Dukedom of Aubigny in France from his grandmother, was MP for Chichester as the Earl of March, and at 18 married in The Hague to settle a gambling debt incurred by his father.

The lucky lady was one Sarah, daughter of the Earl of Cadogan. But immediately after the ceremony he was rushed off on the Grand Tour. Absence, however, really cooled his heart apparently, because on his return he didn't even want to see his wife again and hopped off one night to the theatre.

There, quite coincidentally, would you believe, he saw a beautiful lady who he was told was Lady March, the toast of London. They were re-united, had 12 children and 28 years of marriage, putting up Carne's Seat in the meantime.

From this building Sarah and her daughters spent many happy years enjoying the panoramic views of Sussex and Hampshire, and also seven years in building the Shell House.

This is an escapist and fanciful grotto lined with shells sent back to Goodwood from British sailors throughout the world.

They were happy and charming times of an aristocratic English family untroubled and tranquil in a Sussex countryside idyll.

Goring

Castle Goring lies one and a half miles north of Goring itself and was designed by Biago Rebecca in about 1790 for Sir Bysshe Shelley.

The design is one of the most accurate representations of the taste of that period that can be found anywhere, but also boasts a curious marriage of styles.

The entrance side is Gothic flint and stone with a symmetrical three-towered centre and lower wings.

But the details are unusual for a house of that age, and include dogtooth and chevron ornament, and accurate mouldings. There are also chevrons on perpendicular doors and orders of dogtooth on perpendicular windows.

Immediately through the archways, between centre and wings, the style becomes Graeco-Palladian – the mixture used by architects such as Holland and Bonomi.

Inside, a baronial door leads to a central circular hall with a large glass dome and spiral staircase.

Hammerwood

Hammerwood Park House, near East Grinstead, has seen an astonishing variety of owners in its 191-year history, among them bankers, a clergyman, an Army colonel and a rock band!

In 1973 Led Zeppelin bought the property with the aim of converting it to a massive recording studio with living accommodation for the group and their families.

Plans were drawn up but the dream was never realised as increasing commitments abroad drew the band away and eventually they sold the property. Unfortunately during the nine years the group owned the house vandals removed three tons of lead from the roof and thousands of gallons of water flooded in.

The house was built by Benjamin Latrobe as his first and greatest architectural work in England. Latrobe later emigrated to America, and became architectural adviser to President Jefferson during which time he was put in charge of constructing the Capitol in Washington. He also re-designed the exterior porticos of the White House.

Hammerwood Park was originally commissioned by John Sperling. It was taken over by the Dorrien Magens family who held the property until the 1830s.

Magens Dorrien Magens, a London banker who bought the house, was one of the first men to set up a Home Guard. It consisted of 1,000 men ready to defend the country against the threat of a Napoleonic invasion.

His son, who took over the house, was later responsible for connecting East Grinstead with the railway system at Three Bridges.

During World War Two Hammerwood Park was requisitioned and became the home of 200 soldiers including the cricketer Denis Compton.

Harting

The 17th century mansion of Uppark was suggested when a grateful nation wished to present a country house to the Duke of Wellington after Waterloo.

The Duke was apparently delighted by the idea, and, on July 19, 1816, he wrote on gilt-edged paper to Uppark's owner, Sir Harry Fetherstonhaugh: "From all I have heard and know of Uppark, I should prefer to have that place to any other."

The Duke decided to visit the house, but when he reached Harting and saw the steep road to Uppark on the crest of the South Downs, Wellington calculated that he would have to buy horses for his stables every 18 months, and turned down the house.

The history of the lofty Uppark site, offering magnificent views of the sea beyond Chichester and the Isle of Wight, goes back to Elizabethan times when the deer park was let to a London merchant.

Some of the masonry in the basement of the present house is probably 16th century, and the Sussex Commissioners and the Harting Register have entries of 1591 and 1624 naming retainers of the Ford family "dwelling at Up Park."

The existing red brick house at Uppark was built around 1690, for Forde, Lord Grey of Werke and 1st Earl of Tankerville. He was a leading light in Monmouth's rebellion, who regained his status under James II and William II.

In 1747 the house, with its prominent stone dressings, was bought by Matthew Fetherstonehaugh, who obtained a baronetcy. Together with his wife, he set about redecorating the interior and he filled it with furniture and pictures gained from a grand tour of Europe.

In 1780, Sir Harry brought his mistress, a beautiful Cheshire showgirl of 15 named Emma Hart, to live at Uppark. She twice became pregnant but was discarded in late 1781.

But she did not remain destitute for long, for she later married Sir William Hamilton – and became the notorious mistress of Lord Nelson. In later years, Sir Harry began a "courtly correspondence" once again with Lady Hamilton.

In his youth, Sir Harry was a lavish entertainer, and the Prince Regent was a frequent visitor to Uppark. But in later life, Sir Harry became a recluse and in 1825, when over 70, he married his head dairy-maid.

The building remained in the care of the Fetherstonehaugh family until 1954, when Admiral the Hon. Herbert Meade-Fetherstonehaugh and his son Richard gave the house to the National Trust.

Hastings

The house standing at 31 The Bourne, Hastings, was built in 1450 and is a condensed version of the traditional "three bay" hall design.

Normally in this type of house the hall would occupy the whole of the centre section with the owner's rooms and domestic quarters at either side.

It would also originally have had ladder stairs to the two upper floors of the domestic quarters. They comprised three rooms, one above the other.

The first room encountered on entering the house was the owner's private room, designed exclusively for his or his guest's use.

The fireplace is not contemporary, but was probably added 100 to 150 years later.

Under the floor is a horseshoe-shaped cellar which seems to have been used as a boat pound during the 17th and 18th centuries.

Small craft could travel up the Bourne stream on a flood tide, and then pull up under the front of the house. At the time the stream ran down the centre of the road.

Hastings

One of the disadvantages in delving into the past is that the style of writing in the last century tends to be different from that of today, as Leonard Whyte, who lives in the Old School House, Hastings, discovered.

What started off as a perusal of the deeds ended up with many hours poring over old handwritten documents before they were fully deciphered.

"With the older ones the letter 's' was replaced with 'f' and the writing was difficult to figure out," said Mr Whyte, who has lived there for seven years.

"But it was very enjoyable and the information I gleaned proved very interesting."

Although unable to discover the exact age of the two-storey building, he did find out how the house acquired its name.

A handwritten document, dated 1835, states: "In the Reign of His Majesty King William IV" the house was bought from a Mrs Sarah Milward, widow.

The buyers were the Rev John Googe Foyster, clerk rector of the joint parishes of St. Clement and All Saints in the town and port of Hastings, together with the Rev William Marychurch, of Saint Mary's Chapel, and William Scrivens Esq., mayor of the town.

The three represented the Chichester Diocesan Fund which turned it into a school for boys known as All Saints Church of England School, which it remained until 1869 when the diocesan authority sold it for use as a private dwelling.

Hastings

St. Clement's Church in Hastings owes its present site to Alan the cheesemonger and his wife Alice, who gave the land in 1286.

The gift was presumably welcome, as on its earlier lower site, the church was suffering from the sea's inundations.

St. Clement's was one of the churches that belonged to the Manor of Brede, given to the Abbey of Fecamp in Normandy, and remained in his hands until 1413 when Henry V seized all the possessions of French monasteries in the land.

In 1339 and 1377 the church was badly damaged during French raids. Thus the greater part of the present building dates from 1380.

St. Clement's and its sister church All Saints, across the valley, are the only survivors of medieval Hastings seven churches. They were united under one Rector from 1770 to 1849, and in 1979 formed one parish.

There is the remains of a stoup for holy water on the right hand side of the west door through the tower, and above the entrance are two modern shields of arms of Hastings and the Foyster family, which provided three notable 19th century rectors.

Entering the church and turning left, there is a framed picture and sonnet to the memory of poet and artist Dante Gabriel Rossetti, who married Elizabeth Siddall there on May 23, 1860.

The church tower wall also has a memorial board to the Hon Archibald Hutcheson, MP, who was one of the few who tried to expose the great financial disaster of The South Sea Bubble in 1720.

Hastings

Many summer visitors to Hastings are perplexed by the title of St. Mary-in-the-Castle church.

For the 19th century church, designed and built by Joseph Kay, far from being inside Hastings Castle lies just to the south of it.

The answer to the puzzle lies within the castle itself, where the remains of the original 11th century church can still be found.

The castle was built shortly before 1069 by the Count of Eu and the original church seems to have been begun before 1094, although it saw several additions in the following centuries.

Finally the castle became a crumbling ruin, and Mr Kay stepped in with an ambitious plan for a new church.

He made St. Mary-in-the-Castle the centrepiece for the elegant Pelham Crescent – built in 1824 for the Earl of Chichester.

In recent years the Old Town of Hastings Preservation Society has carried out a major renovation scheme at Pelham Crescent, restoring it to its original state.

Herstmonceux

It is thought that the Brewers' Arms in Herstmonceux is haunted, possibly by witches.

Relatives of the owners swear that they have heard chanting noises at night and the flash of blueish lights.

A typically picturesque Sussex country inn, the Brewers' Arms bears a sign outside which says it dates from the 16th century.

But as church records say the pub dates from the 17th century, and the Department of the Environment lists the building as 18th century, the owners recently took steps to establish an exact origin.

A recognised authority on the history of timber-framed buildings inspected the premises. He found that the centre of the building, originally comprising of two cottages, was present in 1620. The long, slanting roof was added some 200 years later.

The original building was a Tudor-style black and white timber-framed house. The outside of the present building now bears wooden slats and is under restoration.

Inside, there is a largish hole in the beams next to the original inglenook fireplace. It is said that the owners would force a pole into the hole – and tether their children to it to stop them falling into the fire.

Horsham

In towns and villages throughout Sussex, the local inn is often the best reminder of the past.

Every town and most villages have their own watering hole often dating back to the earliest days of the settlement. Horsham is no exception.

The town abounds with historic buildings, and one of the earliest is the Kings Head hotel situated in the centre at The Carfax.

The building is reputed to date from 1401. Now a 28-bedroom hotel, the building has 18th century additions and boasts a Horsham stone roof and extensive cellars.

Legend has it that the building was frequently used by Henry VIII and from that association it took its name.

Horsham

Horsham's nuns were quick off the mark in the 13th century, and their treatment of St. Mary's church bears witness to this.

In 1231, the rights to the early English building passed to nuns at Rusper Priory and they rebuilt almost immediately with a classically simple plan – wide five-bay plain nave, round piers and abaci, double-chamfered arches and a lancet clerestory.

The church undoubtedly dates back considerably further than the Rusper Priory nuns, for although Horsham gets no mention in the 1086 Domesday Book a village certainly existed at that time.

This is not unusual, for the sheer enormity of the task confronting the compilers of the Domesday Book, in a country with at best primitive roads and at times hostile residents, ensured many villages escaped their net.

Its position ensured it later became a trading centre, although this declined so that one report described it as "no more than a village" in 1830.

Before this, Rusper nunnery was suffering itself, and did not survive the dissolution of the monasteries in Henry VIII's reign.

The original Norman church was largely replaced by 1247, although there have been additions since then, mostly in the perpendicular period.

In 1307, the Trinity Chapel was added to the north side and in the 15th century more was added.

Hove

Maples Store in Hove is one of the town's better-known landmarks and forms a fine example of mid-Victorian architecture.

It once supplied the gentry in nearby Palmeira Square and Adelaide Crescent and today stocks furniture, carpets and curtaining.

The building was erected in 1873 as a private house on the instructions of Sir Davigdor Goldsmid, the wealthy Parliamentarian. However, once the property was built Sir Davigdor spent very little time there, preferring to remain abroad.

Thus the place became Palmeira Stores and it was during that period that it supplied local residents and their households.

Maples store itself was originally situated in King's Road in 1907 and stayed there until 1962 when the lease ran out. At that point, it moved to its present premises in Western Road, and the King's Road site eventually became The Cannon public house.

When The Cannon was being built the original Maples store sign came to light.

Hove

The design of Hove public library, in Church Road, came about as a result of an Edwardian competition.

In 1891, Hove's first lending library opened in Grand Avenue and by the next year it had 4,685 books in stock. The library stayed there for ten years until new premises were acquired in Third Avenue.

Both of these houses were adapted for use as a library, and were not purpose built. However, in 1903, Andrew Carnegie made the generous offer of £10,000 to build a new library, provided the site was not a charge on the library rate.

There was a delay in taking up his offer, however, owing to the difficulty of finding a site. The land decided upon in Church Road was only made available by transferring the corporation depot elsewhere.

A competition was set up to decide the design of the building. The response to the first advertisement was disappointing, but the second brought the plan by Percy Robinson and W. Alban Jones of Leeds (who also designed Leeds library), which was adopted.

The front facade has changed little over the years, except that the light stone has darkened, some windows have been replaced and there is an illuminated sign over the original stone.

The cupola over the reference library survived until 1967, when a survey found it to be in a dangerous condition and it was removed.

Behind the straight, Renaissance-style front the building forms a rotunda, with a dome over the hall of the reference library.

In the smaller room of the reference library, there are some attractive wood carvings on the oak bookcases. The motif is of a bay leaf garland above a cluster of fruit and flowers, with tiny acorns as well.

The library was opened on July 8, 1908, by the Countess of Jersey. In the reference library, there is a leather-bound copy of Porter's History of Hove which was probably presented to her. A telegram was sent to Andrew Carnegie thanking him for the "handsome gift of the building."

In the new building, the stock of books increased considerably and in 1908 there were 42,801.

During its early years, the library was a male preserve, but in 1915 (perhaps because so many young men had enlisted) the first woman assistant was employed.

In 1920, a separate children's library was opened in the basement, while story-telling to children was begun in 1921.

Today, the library is a busy place, especially because Hove has a high proportion of retired people.

Hove

During the 18th century, Sussex coastal villages were not renowned as centres for industrial development – but there was one booming trade – smuggling. It also bridged the class barrier, bringing together everyone from squire to ship's hand.

In Hove, the vicar of St. Andrew's church also found himself involved, although whether he was a willing participant is not recorded.

The village used to be a haunt for smugglers running cargoes from Ostend and small towns on the French coast, landing their boats on the shingle under cover of night at the bottom of Hove Street Gap.

Legend has it that the smugglers secreted their booty in the churchyard – thinking that was the one place people were unlikely to wander near after dark.

On one occasion, smuggling took precedence over the church's fortnightly service. The vicar arrived to take the service, and found the bell silent.

When he asked the sexton the reason, he was told the service was due to be held at Preston that day. Eventually the vicar ordered the bell to be rung, whereupon the sexton said: "It's no use, sir, you can't preach today because the church is full of tubs and the pulpit's full of tea."

Hove

Hove owes its most fashionable Christian church to an enterprising Jewish gentleman.

It is the church of St. John the Baptist, as upstanding a corner of the religious establishment as Sussex has.

Yet it took St. John's 112 years to become a parish in its own right. After its speculative birth the church was sold to private enterprise, which in turn led to a strictly unorthodox situation.

Because the church was owned privately and not by the Ecclesiastical Commissioners it meant that church wardens had virtual hire and fire power through a control of the vicarage.

If they'd taken a dislike to their cleric all they had to do was refuse him permission to live in their vicarage to virtually force him out of the pulpit as well. But with true Christian application, they never used their unusual power.

The final granting of an Order in Council by the Privy Council was acknowledgement of the importance to the borough of St. John's and allowed it to become a separate parish in its own right without having to refer business to its mother church of All Saints.

Up until World War One St. John's congregation was a spectator must for the lesser mortals of Hove.

The wealthiest families crowded into the pews on a Sunday and after the requisite enobling address to ensure them, among other things, that their class equality was in the pattern of life they used to walk across the Brunswick Lawns in handmade suits and with the ladies decked out in feather boas, parasoles and the fanciest of gowns.

The first vicar – although they were strictly only called priests-in-charge until the granting of parish status – was one Rev F. Reade, who served St. John's for 40 years from 1854 until 1894.

It was the fourth vicar, the Rev J. S. Flynn, who brought children into the church during his stay there from 1904 for 18 years. He started one of Hove's first children's services.

But children weren't the only visitors. St. John's has also numbered among its congregation Princess Beatrice, daughter of Queen Victoria, and had among its preachers Dean Inge, Dean Matthews and Bishop Gore.

An equivalent stir was created by another vicar, the fifth. He was the Rev A. C. MacNutt and among other structural alterations he thought fit to introduce a cross and candles for the altar.

Popery and "going over to Rome" were the accusations that followed.

St. John's survived them needless to say. And there's no report of vicars before or since being anything but proud of one of Hove's most elegant churches.

Hurstpierpoint

Kents Farmhouse, Hurstpierpoint, dating from the 17th century, is constructed in classic Sussex farmhouse style, half-tiled and with a timber frame.

Kents, still used as a private farm, was built earlier than 1658, since a map of the Danny estate of that date shows the house and farm.

This map includes a drawing of a large tree adjoining the house, near to where a duck pond now lies.

The pond is shown in a plan attached to auction particulars of 1851. The auction was held at the New Inn, Hurstpierpoint. Kents Farm was sold, together with nearby Richman's farm and 87 acres of land, for under £3,000 to the Monk Breton estate.

By the 19th century, the timber-framed original house of Kent's Farm had been extended.

Hurstpierpoint

The 18th century Ruckford Mill, Hurstpierpoint, was converted into a house 20 years ago but still retains many original features and most of the milling machinery.

Much of the present structure dates from around 1768. A plaque in the kitchen, on what was the original eastern wall, bears that date and the inscription NA, which stood for the miller of that time, Nathaniel Avery. However, it is believed that parts of the building are older, and it is known that there were at least two millers before Nathaniel.

The name of Avery appeared again on an Ordnance Survey map of 1843, although by that time a Henry Vunwins had been using the mill for some years. In 1853, he was followed by William Wood, whose descendants used the property until 1909.

During this century the mill was run by Charles Packham Ltd., but milling ceased in 1966.

Much of the milling machinery has been preserved within the building in case owners may want to restore it to working order.

Hurstpierpoint

The former St. Lawrence Church, Hurstpierpoint, was probably of pre-Norman origin and was mentioned in the Domesday Book in 1086.

But the structure, after centuries of additions and alterations, was demolished and rebuilt in the 1840s to become the Holy Trinity Church.

The present church was designed by Charles Barry in a late 13th century early decorated Gothic style.

It was rebuilt following complaints about the structure and size of St. Lawrence Church, which seated only 500 people in a growing parish.

Stone was contributed from the quarry owned by Nathaniel Borrer, father of the Rev Cary Hampton Borrer, the rector of the parish.

Surviving features from the old church include 13th century stone seats for the priests, now in the south transept.

There is also a cross-legged effigy of a knight in 13th century chain armour, and another in late 14th century plate armour.

The latter usually held to represent Simon de Pierpoint, the founder of the original church.

Isfield

The Laughing Fish pub in Isfield, dating from 1861, was once called the Station Hotel and owes its more imaginative current name to a landlord of the 1950s.

He was a former Fleet Street reporter called Tommy Thompson and the story goes that Tommy's friends from London could not imagine him running a pub with the prosaic title of Station Hotel.

So the name was changed to the Laughing Fish, believed to be unique as a pub name in Britain, although one exists in Florida, USA.

Tommy also introduced the East Money Isfield beer race.

Isfield's original pub, more than a century before, was called the Half Moon and was at the other end of the village, opposite the Post Office. But when the railway came in 1857, the pub moved to a site beside the station.

The front outside doors of the Laughing Fish are shaped rather like church doors, and it is believed the building originally was intended as a chapel.

But the Elders of the Chapel ran out of money before it could be finished or consecrated and the building was sold to the brewery.

Itchingfield

Back in 1865 Sir Gilbert Scott undertook a major restoration of Itchingfield's historic church.

While removing the casing from one of the old oak roof beams he made a grisly find.

Sir Gilbert uncovered a human skull, thought to be that of Sir Hector Maclean who fought for the Young Pretender in 1715.

Maclean was a friend of the Rev Alexander Hay, who let him take refuge in the church when the rebellion failed.

But Sir Hector was caught and executed, and his head was placed on a roof beam.

Possibly during the final skirmish before his capture, a bullet was fired in the church, for a careful finger can still find its bed in one of the oak tower posts.

The first Norman church was erected in Itchingfield in about 1125. The north wall, west wall and one of the windows still remain in the present St. Nicholas Church.

The original building forms the present nave of the church, with the east wall where the present screen is, and the south wall where the pillars stand between the nave and the south aisle.

Also original are the hinges and ironwork on the door into the vestry, though the oak door had to be replaced in 1866.

Soon after 1330 a tower was added to the west end with a belfry, and the framework is held together by four enormous oak beams, each 20 inches square.

To the south west of the church is a fascinating example of medieval architecture, known as The Priest's House. it goes back to Itchingfield parish's connection with Sele Priory near Bramber, which is recorded as far back as 1235.

To collect tithes from the area a monk would ride through the forest from Sele, stay overnight and celebrate mass there before returning the next day.

A permanent lodging for him was erected in the late 1400s. It was two storeys high and forms the eastern half of the present building.

In 1536 King Henry VIII dissolved Sele Priory and the building became an almshouse with the western annexe added in about 1600.

Kingston

The Juggs Arms, at Kingston, near Lewes, has the appearance of a typical Sussex country inn.

However the Grade II listed building, which dates back to the 15th century, was originally a farmhouse and has only been a pub since the mid-1950s.

The pub's unusual name is taken from the jugget women who used to carry juggets or baskets of fish on their heads on a path along the Downs from Brighton to the market at Lewes.

A new and specially-commissioned pub sign showing a jugget lady in 18th century costume was painted in 1984.

The inn is in 15th century timber-framed style in English oak. It also used to have a thatched roof but this was replaced with tiles some two centuries ago.

The upper exterior frontage is tile-hung and, below this, brickwork has been added then whitewashed over. Two dormer windows were added in Victorian times but an original grilled window survives on the upper floor.

The building was used as a farmhouse until 1877, and was in private use until the 1950s.

Lewes

It was King Henry VIII's dissolution of the monasteries that earned Anne of Cleves house its name.

At that time, land and buildings belonging to Lewes priory were turned over to the King's right hand man, Thomas Cromwell.

Cromwell was one of the prime movers in splicing Henry with Anne of Cleves, and when the marriage fell through he was digraced.

As a consequence, his land went principally into making up Anne's divorce settlement.

It was on that land that the present timber-framed Anne of Cleves house was built around 1530.

In 1599, a stone porch and an east wing were added. The inscribed date can still be seen on the porch.

Further buildings were added to the back of the house during the 17th century, including one room without a fireplace but unusually well lit for the period.

Windows, above average size for Elizabethan tastes, let light into the room that is believed to have been a weaving workshop.

Anne of Cleves house, in Southover High Street, is now a local history museum, having been given to the Sussex Archaeological Society by the Verral family in 1920.

The society restored the three-storey house to the condition it would have been in 450 years ago.

Lewes

Uckfield solicitor Charles Dawson rocketed to fame when in 1912 he announced to the world that he had discovered the missing link between man and ape.

But the considerable kudos he received was soon overshadowed by the controversy that eventually exposed Dawson's 500,000-year-old man as the bones of an immature orang-utan.

What has never been made clear was whether Dawson himself was the hoaxer, or whether he had been duped into finding the supposed fossil. The site of his find soon became a household name, and The Piltdown Man was known to millions.

But if Dawson made enemies with the Piltdown Man find, he previously made even more bitter foes of the Sussex Archaeological Society with an amazing piece of professional skulduggery.

For at the annual meeting of the society in 1904, the chairman announced that not only had Dawson bought their HQ, Castle Lodge in Lewes, but he had also served them with notice to quit.

To say the members were astonished would be an understatement, for they had understood if the property was to be sold they would have the option of purchasing.

Indeed, many believed the vendors were under the impression that Dawson, being a solicitor, was acting on behalf of the society.

A measure of the feeling running among the society's members can be gleaned from a history of the group by Mr L. Salzman. In a footnote reference to Dawson, he says: "Mr Dawson's name was later given to the Piltdown Man – the lowest form of human being, with the discovery of whose remains he was associated."

It seems Dawson may have been motivated in part by love, for he married soon after and he and his bride moved into Castle Lodge.

Lewes

The Crown Hotel in Lewes, which overlooks the town's war memorial, once used to gaze out at a far more lively scene. For that spot was where the cattle market was held, and while farmers were busy bargaining, the landlord and his staff were inside preparing lunch.

When this was ready a waiter would stand outside the gates and ring a large bell – and then presumably stand well clear to escape the rush!

Since the days of the Stuarts, The Crown ranked as one of the three leading hostelries in the town. It is said that William IV, when in residence at the Brighton Pavilion, paid some incognito visits there. At one stage the building went through a period of decline, although this has now been largely rectified with extensive alterations to the interior.

In the course of the alterations, a small brown jug and three clay pipes, all well over 200 years old, were discovered embedded in the foundations of a wall.

The original name of the inn was the Black Lion. In 1675 the landlord was a Henry Townsend, while in 1771 the host boasted the appropriate name of Malt. It was in 1790 that the landlord of the day, Joseph Spittle, changed its name to The Crown.

Lewes

Sculptor Auguste Rodin's erotic masterpiece, The Kiss, was commissioned by American art collector Edward Warren when he owned the historic Lewes House in Lewes High Street.

This major work was displayed officially in the town for only two years and was later removed on the grounds of taste! Now it is one of the Tate Gallery's most prized exhibits.

Frenchman Rodin was one of the many Bohemian friends and visitors of the rich and cultivated Warren. They included members of the Bloomsbury group.

The Kiss was completed in 1906 and brought to Lewes, but because of its larger-than-life size and weight was placed in the coach-house.

In 1914 Warren offered it to the town for display and for just over two years it had pride of place in Lewes Town Hall.

When Rodin died in 1917 the borough council, fearing that the theme of the statue (an embracing couple) might have an "undesirable effect" upon local residents, asked Warren to take it back.

It was returned to its home in the coach-house where it remained for more than ten years until Warren died in 1928.

The statue changed hands several times between then and 1939 when it was loaned to the Tate Gallery, which bought it in 1955 for a "token" £7,500. Now it is regarded as priceless.

References to Lewes House go back to 1625 while the early Georgian features of the house date from 1733.

In 1949 the building was listed as being of architectural and historic interest and in 1974 came under the ownership of Lewes District Council, whose principal offices are housed there.

The rooms of the house are not open to the public but visitors can view the garden on the south side of the building. There is also a small collection of Edward Warren memorabilia which can be viewed on appointment with the district secretary.

Lewes

The White Hart Hotel in Lewes was perhaps justifiably dubbed The Cradle of American Independence after rights campaigner Tom Paine started frequenting it.

For it was at the White Hart, in 1768, that Paine formed the Headstrong Club, along with several other stalwarts from the town.

At the time he was an Excise Officer living at Bull House, but as the club continued to meet in the elegant panelled rooms, Paine felt the American cause drawing him overseas.

A few years later he left Lewes and went across the Atlantic, where he established a formidable reputation for himself as a revolutionary and humanitarian.

Years later Paine, with his fervour still bright, maintained Lewes – and especially the White Hart Hotel – was the "Cradle of American Independence".

About 150 years after its association with Tom Paine, the hotel played another important role in world history.

The talks between the then British Foreign Secretary, Arthur Henderson, and the envoy of the USSR, Dougalovsky, took place in 1929 and culminated in the resumption of British diplomatic relations with Russia.

The original building dates back to the 14th century and was for many years the family seat of the Pelhams, until in 1717 they moved across the road and the buildings became a famous coaching inn.

Lindfield

Living in Firs Cottage at Lindfield is a dangerous affair – if you take notice of old superstitions that is.

Long ago, before the National Health Service offered its somewhat shaky pharmaceutical shield of protection over the nation's well-being, staying fit was largely a question of keeping your fingers crossed on the one hand and keeping on the right side of ancient lore on the other.

So it was that the tradition came about of building houses all facing what historians seem to think was the north-east. Whether it kept the draught from prevailing winds out, or whether the medieval gods were thus appeased, we'll never know.

But this was the general rule of the times and builders were generally supposed to keep to it. One place though where they simply didn't bother was Firs Cottage. Since about 1500 it has faced defiantly south.

But surprise, surprise, illness doesn't seem to have visited here any more than any other house facing other points.

Could it be that bad luck was a visitor here in another guise? The last man reputed to have been hanged in Sussex lived there before he killed a member of his family and paid the full penalty.

Now the old cottage is more than respectable.

Cottage, in fact, is possibly a misnomer. It's two cottages rolled into one and the property has five bedrooms among its modernised offerings.

Construction is with small Tudor bricks and in the parlour there is a wide chimney corner and a brick oven.

The bedrooms contain ships' timbers which still have the peg holes and slots from their original usage.

The property takes its name from an old manor house which burnt down and is now only a memory.

Lindfield

The Toll House at Lindfield was once, as its name still implies, a cash collecting house where travellers paid for the privilege of riding the rocky road that ran through the village.

A plaque outside the shop says that the building ended the toll part of its life in October 1884. For Lindfield that wasn't soon enough. Once there were two toll houses at either end of the village and it cost travellers a right royal 6d to get from one side to the other – a hefty price in those days.

One William Ansell recorded it all in some parish accounts of 1858 and told how the resultant cash was used for the general upkeep of the village and, of course, the road through it.

In 1861 there was a meeting in a local public house called the Tiger in which local residents called for an end to the travel levy. A petition was signed by 19 residents and they were unanimous in dubbing the toll houses a collective nuisance.

But it wasn't until the spring of 1884 that the bell of progress tolled an end for the toll.

Lower Beeding

Life must have been pretty busy for the man steering London's flagship department store Harrods through the hectic 1920s and depressed 1930s.

So when things became too much for Sir Woodman Burbidge and his wife Cissily they hopped into the Rolls and popped down to Lower Beeding in Sussex.

But despite the hard work, being chairman of Harrods had its compensations as Sir Woodman wasn't slow to appreciate.

He had the Cisswood House, Lower Beeding, built especially in 1928, and when it came to the wood and plaster work – who else but Harrods' craftsmen could do the job?

One of his chief rural pursuits was coursing with whippets, and he kept several of the animals at Cisswood House.

The house is built in mock Tudor style, which was typical of the popular style of the late 1920s and early 1930s.

Lower Beeding

It was supposed to be nine feet long with bunches at its side looking like footballs. And the people who saw it were worried that the bunches would change into wings!

Plainly IT was the dragon monster of Lower Beeding, rapacious, horrific and luckily not seen much this side of the Middle Ages.

Those centuries ago in wild areas like the St. Leonard Forest beasties were not that uncommon. On this occasion history says it was "the Horsham carrier and the other three" who saw the creature and later reported that its principal food was luckless neighbourhood rabbits.

Needless to say, sightings were the only sketchy offer by way of proof. Later years also produced sceptics who wondered if the Horsham carrier hadn't caught a glimpse of an over-large water snake that may have been dwelling in one of the area's many hammer ponds.

But such are the stories that helped make the forest thickets and glades more mysterious – and Lower Beeding, where the forest extended, a delightful setting today for houses like Old Woldringfold.

Originally it is likely that the Saxon name for the locality was Beding and in the Domesday Book there is a reference to Beddinges. Romans were also here and about 150 years ago a tumulus brim-full of urns was unearthed.

At the time of the Conquest, the woods provided abundant fuel for smelting and it wasn't long before Norman lords were combing the forest for more reliable monsters like wild boar. Then the boundaries were close to those of Lower Beeding.

Until the year 1837 buck and doe were given annually in lieu of tithes. But later two churches were built in the forest and a rent imposed on the cultivated land for the incumbent's maintenance.

And where does Upper Beeding fit into it all? The parishes were split in 1838 and are ten miles apart. Lower Beeding sits loftily at some height compared with sea level, while Upper Beeding resides in a river valley – an example of geographical naming perversity if ever there was one.

Mayfield

One of the most spectacular medieval halls in England is housed in the former Old Palace of the Archbishops of Canterbury at Mayfield.

The hall, built around 1325, became ruined during the late 18th century. But it was restored in the 1860s and is used as a chapel by the Convent of the Holy Child, who now occupy the Old Palace.

The earliest English remains of the palace date from the late 13th century. The spacious Great Hall was built by Archbishop Reynolds between 1313 and 1327 and was undoubtedly one of the finest in the kingdom.

Built of local sandstone, the most striking features of the hall are its pointed transverse stone arches which run across.

They are said to be the widest stone arches built in the medieval period, and spring from corbels on short shafts supported by grotesque figures.

The Archbishop's residence reached the climax of its glory in the mid-14th century.

Archbishops of the later 15th century did not live at Mayfield and its fortunes began to decline.

However, the last of the Catholic lords, William Warhan revived its glories. The addition of the fine Gate House and the porch of the Great Hall is attributed to him.

In the 17th and 18th centuries, the property changed hands several times and fell into disrepair. The final blow came when Michael Baker, who died in 1759, had the hall dismantled, its roof stripped off and stones removed.

In 1863 a party of children from a convent school founded by Mother Connelly at St. Leonards spent the day at the site, and were stunned by the beauty of the ruins.

A rich woman, the Duchess of Leeds, got to hear of the visit. She resolved to buy the property and present it to the Society of the Holy Child Jesus on condition that the ruins be restored.

Within two years, sufficient funds were collected among Catholics to begin the restoration, and on July 21, 1865, Mass was celebrated in the Great Hall, now a chapel.

Michelham Priory

Legend has it that Thomas Backett, a close friend of the Aquila family of Pevensey Castle, nearly met with a watery death in the mill stream at Michelham Priory.

He was pitched into the stream while out hunting with his friend Gilbert d'Aquila, but was saved when the sluices miraculously closed.

A wealth of history surrounds the priory. It was built in the 13th and 14th centuries on a site in the Sussex low Weald, which was surrounded by thick oak forest and within a great bend in the River Cuckmere.

In fact, its location gives rise to the name of the place – in the Anglo Saxon "Michel hamm" means water meadow.

Whether the site was always an island, as it is now, is unclear, but the western gatehouse side of the moat is considered to have been part of the main river system.

Michelham was a monastery of Austin Canons, one of six in Sussex, where a community of men devoted their life to prayer.

The 60ft high Gateway Tower was built by Prior Leem in about 1395, and is largely in original condition today. It is faced with Eastbourne greensand covering walls of chalk and flint more than four feet thick.

On either side of the entrance arch were the porters' rooms, with the original stone stairway leading to the two upper floors and roof in the small south east corner turret.

Midhurst

Midhurst, like so many other Sussex hamlets, is a place where history abounds. The village was once built around a typical late medieval design.

It has four streets leading from its centre along the main compass points. Hardly surprisingly, these were called North, South, East and West Street.

One of the more charming properties in the village is located in West Street, and the lease is owned by M. W. Blackiston the butcher.

The shop has been a butcher's – used by the Blackiston family – since 1900, when the present leaseholder's grandfather moved in. The building itself dates back to 1660 and forms part of the Cowdray Estate. The bow-fronted window to the shop was added in the early 1960s after a fire extensively damaged the building.

Midhurst

Midhurst Grammar School has, in it's 314 year history, seen many ups and downs.

Formed in 1672 by the prominent weaver and coverlet maker Gilbert Hannam, the school aimed to give 12 "poor boys" a chance to learn the three Rs as well as Latin and Greek.

The school was originally sited in the loft of the Market House, near the church, and later moved to its present North Street site.

But during the following two centuries, Hannam's wishes were severely frustrated, mainly through the neglect of its governing body.

In common with many grammar schools in the 18th century, Midhurst tottered near ruin and from 1700-10, under the Rev Richard Oliver, things reached such a pitch that local people presented a petition to the trustees.

The Rev Everard Levitt, 1717-35, attracted a similarly outraged response and the Rev Francis Atkins, 1758-88, was accused of pocketing the school funds.

The reforming zeal of the 19th century helped save the school, and under the Rev John Wooll, 1799-1807, it achieved fame and prosperity.

Wooll's abilities were recognised outside Sussex, for his next post after Midhurst was Rugby school.

But as the century progressed the school's fortunes began to slide again, mainly under the headmastership of the Rev William Goodenough Bayly.

The curriculum was considered outdated with its concentration on Greek and Latin to the exclusion of almost everything else. During that time the number of pupils at the school declined to one – hardly surprisingly that solitary child then ran away.

As a result, the school closed in 1859 and was not re-opened until 1880 under a scheme drawn up by the Charity Commissioners providing places for six Hannam scholars whose fees were paid.

The school at that stage had had enough of the church taking a hand and the curriculum was replaced with a study course, including geography, natural science, music and a European language.

One of the school's more notable pupils was a young H. G. Wells who came to Midhurst as an apprentice to a chemist.

Newtimber

If ever there was a good reason for making a moat, they had one at Newtimber Place, the Elizabethan-style house nestling just under the Downs near Hassocks.

It wasn't for defence, or to start rust in invading chain mail. But because there was a stream and two ponds to start with. And someone back in history had an eye for beauty.

The plot of land that is now Newtimber was first mentioned in the Domesday Book as being part of Poynings. The land and buildings then on it were owned by Lewes Priory. Under the Dissolution by Henry VIII they fell into the hands of Anne of Cleves and subsequently Thomas Cromwell.

The house was rebuilt much as it is now in 1698. It was bought in 1901 by Lord Buxton, a former Liberal MP for Peterborough, Governor General of South Africa, Post-master-General and President of the Board of Trade. He lived at Newtimber until his death.

Normanshurst

Sussex has had a fair share of distinguished men, so for one to gain the title of The Grand Old Man of Sussex would indicate he had some very special qualities.

But that title was just one of many Tom Brassey acquired during his lifetime from 1836 to 1918.

One of the more lasting reminders of the man is the Brassey Institute built for him as a home in the style of his Renaissance-type chateau at Normanshurst.

The chateau has been demolished but the Brassey Institute still goes strong.

It was built in 1879 and designed by the architect W. L. Vernon. It features a mosaic of the Bayeux Tapestry on the front porch.

It originally housed accommodation for rowing club galleys in the basement and a library on the ground floor.

The first floor houses assembly rooms, while the second was used for his private suite and the third floor for a school of art with large north facing skylights.

Lord Brassey, as he became, was Liberal MP for Hastings and opened his library to the public in 1881. He gave the entire building to the town in 1887.

The school of art moved out in 1982 and the museum moved to larger premises in 1928. Now the building is used only for the library service.

Tom Brassey was the eldest of three sons of a Victorian railway contractor. He became a seaman and promoted the cause of the navy in Parliament.

He became Lord Warden of the Cinque Ports from 1908-13, the Mayor of Bexhill from 1906-7 and was Governor-General for Victoria, Australia, from 1895-1900.

With these achievements behind him, it is hardly surprising that the unofficial title of The Grand Old Man of Sussex was also added to the list.

Northiam

The distinctively L-shaped Hayes Arms Hotel, Northiam, was once a 15th century farmhouse. It was extended with a new wing around 1800.

The contrasting Tudor and Georgian aspects of this country house hotel are apparent from the exterior, which stands in its own heavily-wooded grounds. On one side it adjoins the village green and on the other a 12th century church.

The Hayes even boasts a royal connection for in 1573 a meal for Queen Elizabeth I was cooked in the bake-oven of one of its fireplaces.

Two hundred years later, in 1757, Capt Snelling, Molly Bealles and several of their friends visited the house, and as a memento of their visit they scratched their names on a window pane in the bedroom, now named Capt Snelling. Other bedrooms are also named after the revellers.

In the original Tudor section of the house, large inglenook fireplaces, low beams, leaded windows and crooked floors add an authentic atmosphere.

The Georgian wing houses an elegant dining room with twin bay windows overlooking the lawns.

Petworth

Somerset Hospital in Petworth was built as a grand private house by the Mose family in the early 17th century, and bought by the Duke of Somerset in 1728.

Then, in January 1747, the Duke endowed the premises and other property to trustees to found an almshouse.

The property is not quite in the usual Petworth style. It is built of brick and stone, with two bow windows and a taller three-storeyed brick centre.

The original endowment was for 12 widows, each to receive £10 a year. This was increased in 1818 to 22 widows each receiving £20.

The trustees also paid out pensions to 30 other widows of between £10 and £25 a year.

Pevensey

Glyndley Manor, now a magnificent country house hotel, was built in 1508, the year before Henry VIII came to the throne, while the name Glyndley or Glenleigh first appeared as one of the landmarks on a Saxon charter in 947 AD.

The area also gave its name to the family "de Glindlee," members of whom figure in deeds of the 13th century. In 1320, it was named as one of the districts of the Cinque Ports Libert of Pevensey, and there is evidence that a Saxon house stood on the site as far back as 600 AD.

The present manor, set in 17 acres of picturesque Parkland, has been owned by a number of families, but at one time it was used as a nunnery.

It is also said that Anne of Cleves made a long stay in the house, while in more recent times Prince Charles has visited the manor, too.

Polegate

Filching Manor, Polegate, was built around the year 1450 and has been the home of several well-known Sussex families.

There are timbers in the building, particularly in the roof, which come from an even earlier house which seems to have existed on the site.

The basis of the present house consists of the great hall, a ladies' withdrawing room and a solar room above this.

Details of the earliest owners of the manor are not clear but from 1537 several respected county families have lived here.

They included the Fennels, the Markwicks and then Robert Rochester and his son, Charles, whose monument is in Jevington Church and who was married in St. Paul's Cathedral.

The house must have formerly had a stone floor as it seems from smoke-blackened timbers in the roof that there was once a fire in the middle of the hall.

The early medieval doorway contains a door which is reputed to be the oldest original door in an English private house.

The fireplace in the ladies' withdrawing room dates from 1450 while the oak panelling in the hall is of a very early type.

Ringmer

The history of The Cock Inn at Ringmer gives a clue to the origins of the nursery rhyme, Ride a Cock Horse.

For the building was once a substantial inn with expensive stabling and provided a valuable relay post for wagons making their way to Tunbridge Wells from the coast.

At The Cock, the horse teams hitched up a "cock-horse" to provide extra pulling power on the long haul to Tunbridge Wells. The horse, which was hired by the driver of the team, was returned to the landlord on the return journey.

Further evidence of this is provided by the stables which were housed where the car park now stands.

The building itself was constructed in the 16th century and in its time has served food and refreshment to travellers and locals alike.

Rottingdean

Challoner's, Rottingdean's picturesque 15th century manor house, is the oldest dwelling in the village. It occupies one of the highest points and dates from 1456 when Rottingdean was no more than a single, narrow little street leading down to the Gap.

Thomas Challoner built the original manor house on the site of a medieval yeoman's cottage. But only the cellars remain today.

It 1541 it became the property of Hugh Ockenden and towards the end of that century the house, as it now stands, began to take shape.

By 1591 the main part of the house had been completed. The external walls are of random flint and are framed by Spanish oak partitions, beams and roof timbers.

Many ship's timbers are featured – from the Spanish Armada, so the story goes.

From the 17th century to 1915 the house passed into the hands of the Beard family.

Just after the outbreak of the First World War Challoner's was bought by William Brown, who had occupied the house as a tenant for 32 years.

In later years the land and buildings were sold and the house and one acre of garden divided into two.

Challoner's has secret passages which lead from its ancient cellars down to the beach. These have now been largely blocked up.

There is a superb mulberry tree in the garden. It is said to be the largest in the South of England and planted in the reign of James II.

Rottingdean

Building with a dual personality is St. Margaret's Church, in Rottingdean. There is a replica 8,000 miles away in California.

The original church is an impressive building, of flint construction with a squared central tower dating from the 13th century. The other in true American style, is a "faithful reproduction."

It even has postcards with the logo: "A reproduction of the ancient Parish Church of St. Margaret in Rottingdean, England, where Rudyard Kipling worshipped."

The American church however, bears a different name. It is called the Church of the Recessional, and is at Forest Lawn Memorial Park in Glendale, California.

At the Rottingdean church the nave is Norman, as part of one north window shows inside, and foundations have been found which also seem to date from that period.

Much of the church dates from the last century; it was restored by Sir G. Scott in 1856, and the church boasts seven stained glass windows designed by Sir Edward Burne-Jones.

Burne-Jones had a house in the village from 1880 until his death. The finest of his legacy of windows, the Tree of Jesse and Jacob's Ladder, are in the tower.

Rottingdean

Whipping Post House in Rottingdean was built in about 1583 and harks back to the days when brutal punishment was meted out for even the most minor offences.

The practice of public flogging dates back to the Saxon times, but in 1530 Henry VIII passed the Whipping Act which decreed offenders would be tied to the back of carts for their punishment.

Later, posts were set up for this purpose, with the proviso that the "body shall be bloody" before the punishment stopped.

Parents of illegitimate children, prostitutes, dishonest tradesmen and petty thieves all ran the risk of public flogging.

The post in Rottingdean stood outside this property, although these days a chestnut tree stands on the site to give a rather more gentle reminder of the past.

Over the years, Whipping Post House has seen its share of controversy: It was once the home of the notorious local smuggler Captain Dunk.

It is one of the many properties in the village with cellars for hiding contraband, and tunnels which led to the beach.

Rusper

For 200 years, until the early 19th century, Avery's, at Rusper, was the house of the village blacksmith.

The forge, next to the house, remained until early this century, when it was demolished.

Avery's was built around 1550, a timber-framed hall house. A deed of 1553 records that it formed part of the property of John Owen of Wotton, and that it was known as "Owen's Land."

In the early 17th century a front wing was added, the hall divided into two floors and the central chimney stack inserted.

Bricks replaced the original wattle-and-daub infilling, although two original panels remain.

The improvements were made by John Avery, who died in 1630, although the house was not generally known as Avery's until the next century.

After the early 19th century, Avery's was divided up and leased to various tenants, including a butchers and a grocers. But by the latter part of the century, it had reverted to single use again and was the home of yet another tradesman – the miller, Benjamin Jupp.

When Rusper windmill burnt down in 1893 he placed a steam mill in Avery's barn and the woodwork for the machinery remains.

Rye

The Friars of the Sack came to Rye on the crest of a gigantic religious wave that swept England in the 13th century.

The event was known as the Coming of the Friars and involved the followers of St. Francis and St. Dominic, who, during the latter half of the century, brought new ideas through the known world.

The order was officially known as the Brothers of Repentance of Jesus Christ, but the locals doubtless found this rather a mouthful.

Instead they preferred to call them the Friars of the Sack, after the sackcloth they wore.

The order was established in Rye in 1257 and in 1263 the brothers took up residence in a house in Church Square.

Here they were granted permission, if they could find others who were interested, to found a chantry.

The Order ceased to exist in 1307 and the building was used for secular purposes after that date although new floors and roof had to be built after a disastrous fire in 1377.

After the friars left the house it must, in later years, have been quite a bargain to rent. Records of 1670 show that 4d. a year was charged.

Rye

James Lamb (1693-1756) was evidently a man who believed in having the best of both worlds. For while he lived in Rye, the entrepreneur managed to trade as a licensed vintner and hold a post as Collector of Customs for Rye and Shoreham.

In 1721, he bought the land on which Lamb House stands from his father-in-law, and completely re-built the old property. The only portion he retained were the spacious cellars – presumably for his professional calling.

Mr Lamb went on to become Mayor of Rye 13 times, and during that period, entertained the King, George I, at his house. The visit, which lasted four days, came as something of a surprise for Lamb, as indeed it did for the King.

It came as Lamb was serving his second term of office in 1726 and when the ship carrying George I from Hanover to England ran ashore at Camber during a severe storm. On hearing the news, Lamb gathered together some of his municipal officers and rode down to the shore to escort the King back to Lamb House. He stayed for three more nights after a heavy snowfall prevented him from leaving the village. The King became godfather to Lamb's son, who was born during the visit.

In 1898, the American novelist Henry James, leased the property, and acquired the freehold in 1900.

James entertained many renowned writers of the day at Lamb House, including Conrad, Wells, Belloc and Kipling. Another who visited it was the young Compton MacKenzie.

Rye

The word historic doesn't quite do justice to the Mermaid Inn at Rye. It conjures up visions of showpiece, hands-off exhibits.

But step inside this hostelry and you're in the biggest, living, working antique around.

Mark you, it dates back to 1420, which wouldn't be bad even if the hotel were a more sedate museum exhibit.

The Mermaid rates as one of the oldest pubs in the country, and has the unique distinction of having won the Queen's Award to Industry.

Enter its panelled bars and four poster original bedrooms and you enter another world.

The Mermaid had its doors open for 150 years when Queen Elizabeth, in 1573, came to Rye to make it Rye Royal.

It was here that the fictional Dr Syn, of Russell Thorndike's novels, was supposed to have frequented, getting up to no good in old smuggling days, and, when threatened, disappearing down still existing secret passages.

You can still even see an Elizabethan toilet – an upstairs hole in the corner of a room, which once led unhygienically straight down to the outside street.

But it was as a centre for smuggling that Rye and The Mermaid made their name. Even John Wesley was wont to comment, when he visited in 1773: "I found the people willing to hear the good word at Rye but they will not part with the accursed smuggling. So I fear our labour will be in vain."

Stories are legion of the Hawkhurst Gang, of John Cobby, hanged in chains on Selsey Isle, and of the Ruxley Gang, based in Rye and Hastings.

It's a far cry from today's hotel bustle – and a thriving tourist trade.

But the excitement – and the profit – live on.

Rye

The Old Borough Arms, in Rye, is built into and forms part of the Old Town Wall. The building, which is thought to date back to around 1750, was originally a pub, although it has not served that purpose since the turn of the century. It is now run as a hotel with licensed restaurant.

The oak-beamed property is Grade II listed and once lay near one of the most notorious parts of Rye . . . Mermaid Street was in those days the brothel area of the town, and The Old Borough Arms one of the numerous drinking dens that surrounded it.

The area where the old pub stood, in The Strand, also saw an early example of racially segregated bars. For each drinking house in the town was frequented by either French or Dutch sailors and few strayed off their own beaten tracks.

Rye

One of Rye's most imposing buildings, the Old Grammar School in the High Street, was built in 1636 by Sir Thomas Peacock. it was described as "a free school in Rye for the better education and breeding of youth in good literature."

On Sir Thomas's death the school was left to the town along with money for its upkeep. Part of this income came from a mortgage on the Mermaid Inn, which was redeemed, curiously, in 1758, when the inn became bankrupt.

The school must have impressed the Victorian novelist Thackeray, for he sent the hero of an unfinished story of 1860, Dennis Duval, "to a famous, good grammar school at Rye."

In 1884, the school came under the control of the Charity Commissioners and became known as Rye Grammar School, closing in 1907 with completion of a new building. In later years the school was used by Rye Conservative and Working Men's Club, and it is now used to sell fancy goods.

The fascade of the old school has been praised as a masterpiece of brickwork, and compared to like work at Kew Palace. The rendering of classical features in plain and cut brick is felt to be the work of a master, and the front is bound together by the use of giant pilasters.

Rye

The Old Hospital in Mermaid Street, Rye, was at one stage the most expensive "hotel" in the town. But its residents were none too keen to prolong their stay.

For the "guests" were French prisoners of war, captured during the Napoleonic Wars and held there pending payment of ransom money.

It is thought that the present name for the building came from those days, when the place was referred to as a hospice. There are no records of it ever being used as a hospital.

The property, once known as Hartshorne House, seems to date from the early Tudor times, and the height and size of the rooms indicate it was probably the home of a prosperous merchant.

The reign of Elizabeth I brought a new age of luxury and the Old Hospital benefited with plaster carving and panelling, carried out or influenced by craftsmen from Flanders and Italy.

The scholar Samuel Jeake lived there after his marriage to Elizabeth Hartshorne in 1681 and described the building as "the best house in town."

Miss Hartshorne was just 13 years old when she wed Mr Jeake, but three years later bore him a son.

Their fourth child, also named Samuel, was born in 1697 and eventually inherited the house. He studied aeronautics and was evidently a thinker ahead of his time.

One of his achievements was to build a "flying machine", which history tells us failed to achieve its aim and was then stored in the attic of the old grammar school.

St. Leonards

The North Lodge in St. Leonards has played host to literary figures since it was built by James Burton in 1830.

Soon after World War One the author Sir Henry Rider Haggard (1856-1925) lived there and is said to have used as his study the room which forms an archway over the road.

The author, who was an expert on African affairs, captured the imagination of young and old alike with his book King Solomon's Mines in 1885. He followed this two years later with She and further African stories, notably Allan Quartermain and Nada the Lily.

It is possible that while living in St. Leonards, Sir Henry was working on The Queen of the Dawn, a novel about ancient Egypt which was published in 1925.

When he was not writing, he managed to find time to serve on several government commissions connected with agriculture, and for this work he was knighted in 1912.

The author Stephen Potter, who wrote Gamesmanship, also lived at North Lodge for several months in 1925 while working as a private tutor.

It is clear from some of Potter's writings that Rider Haggard made his mark at the house, for Potter describes the place as the Assegai Haunted House. The property was intended to form part of a development designed as a sort of mini-Brighton.

St. Leonards

Most hotels have had one or two visitors leave without paying, but the Royal Victoria in St. Leonards will never forget one particular rogue.

He booked into the hotel in 1851 under the rather unenterprising name of "Mr Smith" and proceeded to run up a bill wining and dining.

Eventually he vanished, and the manager called in the local constabulary. Mr Smith turned out to be the Duke of Brunswick!

And the aristocrat had made good his escape in a hot air balloon. He was probably the first cheat in history to use that form of getaway transport.

During the last century the hotel was a popular haunt for many of the nobility and famous figures – although they were rather more honest about paying the bill than the flamboyant Duke.

The hotel was originally called the St. Leonards Hotel but changed its name to the Royal Victoria after royal patronage. It seems certain that Queen Victoria visited both as a Princess and after ascending to the throne.

The visitors book – kept in a glass case in the reception hall – reads like a copy of Debrett's and is an autograph hunter's dream. The guests even included the poets Tennyson and Wordsworth.

Sheffield Park

Sheffield Park entered the history books in 1264 when Simon de Montfort halted his army at nearby Fletching Common on the eve of the Battle of Lewes.

His victory at Lewes the next day, however, was followed by a disastrous defeat at Evesham the following year, and after the baron's death in battle the manor passed to William Bardolph.

The manor was acquired by the West family in 1299. The Lords de la Warr held it until the mid 15th century when it was seized by the ever acquisitive Henry VI.

Little is recorded of the various tenants and owners of the property over the next 300 years, though it is known that one of them, John Wilson, willed the lease to his son on his deathbed.

It was done on the condition that his widow retained full possession of two rooms . . . "one being the chamber wherein we usually lodge, and with full libertye of accesse, agresse and regresse in, and to and from, the said rooms at all times for her and her servants with lyke libertye to walk and recreate herself at all times in the gallerye."

In the 18th century, the manor was, once again, in full occupation, and comes to the fore again when sold to John Baker Holroyd for £30,000 in 1769.

Holroyd, who died in 1821, was an MP and president of the Board of Agriculture and subsequently became Baron Sheffield and Earl of Sheffield.

The third Earl of Sheffield brought an unusual distinction to the place. He was a keen cricketer and organised the first visits to the country by the Australian Test teams. For many years the opening game was played at Sheffield Park.

The present gardens were laid out by Lancelot Capability Brown, subsequently extended by Arthur Soames when he acquired the property in 1909.

Sheffield Park

One of the top ten tourist attractions in Sussex, the charming Bluebell Railway, stands as a living monument to the glorious heyday of the steam train.

The five mile rural stretch of track, in the heart of the Sussex Weald – from Sheffield Park to Horsted Keynes – was saved by members of the Bluebell Preservations Society in 1959, after British Railways closed the line the previous year.

The Society was the first in the world to take on the job of saving and operating a length of standard gauge passenger railway.

It now boasts restored engines and rolling stock from all over Britain, and celebrated its 25th anniversary this year with the purchase of its 31st steam engine, No. 80064, built in 1953 at the now defunct Brighton works.

People often wonder why the railway is called Bluebell. It is because the line, once part of a secondary track between East Grinstead and Lewes, runs through Sussex countryside which blooms with a haze of bluebells in May.

The two oldest engines in the Bluebell collection, Stepney and Fenchurch, date back to the 1870s, but the stations and equipment are not without their interest, dating back to the construction of the line in 1882.

At Sheffield Park at the southerly edge of the line, the pre-1923 flavour of the London, Brighton and South Coast railway is still strong, with oil-lit platform lamps adding period atmosphere.

Here there is a collection of historic locomotives and a museum of small items connected with the Bluebell Line.

To many people, the rural charm of the Bluebell Railway brings back memories of the "Thomas the Tank Engine" tales of the Rev Wilbert Awdry, who based one of his stories around a Bluebell favourite Stepney, built in 1872.

Shoreham

The earliest documentary mention of St. Nicholas Church, in Shoreham, has been traced as far back as 1075, although the building certainly dates to Saxon times. The 1075 date is interesting for historians, as it falls midway between the Norman Conquest in 1066, and the Domesday Book of 1086.

Records show that in 1075, St. Nicholas was among a package of ecclesiastical properties given to the Abbey of Saumur. It seems unlikely to be accidental that the church now resembles an important village church in Normandy – clearly the monks created a corner of France in this English town.

The date on which the original church was built is harder to trace, although it has been estimated very roughly as "before 900". The other important period in the life of the church came in 1830 when the Cambridge Camden Society carried out a thorough restoration.

Slaugham

Slaugham Manor is about as near an architectural hotch-potch as Sussex offers.

It nestles not far from Handcross, a wedge of greenery between the expansion of Crawley and the development of the South Coast.

The style of this imposing building is Elizabethan. But the date is 1899. It was then that a master builder took it upon himself to discard the services of an architect and to rebuild for the well known Sussex family of Sergison the style of house that had been the centre of the Slaugham estate.

The original house was known as Slaugham Place and today only the barest ruins are still visible behind the thriving hotel that is the current Slaugham Manor.

It was built by Sir Richard Covert, a member of a local family of distinction in the 16th and 17th centuries. Fire is the reputed cause of its dissolution, but from its historical ruins the replacement building saw its beginnings.

The discarded materials from its structure were used to lay the foundations of Slaugham Manor and the imitation style completed a bridge of the centuries.

Not that the manor is that contemporary in building techniques. Its bricks were individually hand-made in wood-fired kilns and its master builder added other individual characteristics too.

It was complicated when a ballroom and conference suite extension were built. The outside was completed in the same mock Elizabethan style but the window mullions were so distinctive that new ones had to be cast in situ on the site itself.

The inside was equally a problem when the manor finally went out of private possession in 1959 – for the exterior Elizabethan facade gave way to a decidedly heavy Victorian interior.

Southwick

A 17th century house overlooking Southwick Green once nestled close to a structure more suited to an Asian dream than a Sussex village. The red-tiled building was designed along the lines of an Indian temple, and was known to the locals as the Buddhist Temple.

In fact, it was built on the orders of an eccentric Englishwoman, Lady Westerney, who was married to an Indian and Buddhist. She lived at Ivy Lodge until she was 86, when she moved to a nursing home. After her death, her ashes were scattered in the Ganges.

The temple was a series of great halls inside, one above the other, with the top-most room adorned with hand painted murals. The middle room windows were of Indian design, with coloured glass. At one end of the room was a marble dias, with supports for a canopy of gold cloth. The decoration of the walls showed some startling incongruities, partly Indian and partly Parisian music hall, depicting chubby cupids reclining on rose beds.

During the war, while Indians were stationed in Brighton, they used the building for meditation and prayer. Sadly, this modern-day planning officer's nightmare has now been demolished, but the remaining farmhouse still boasts some unusual features.

Lady Westerney acted as her own designer, but with the help of a local builder added oak beams and an oak fireplace. She then gave the place a Dutch feel with red tiled ceiling and tiled fireplace and stove.

Stansted

Stansted House lies in splendid, tree-lined grounds on the Sussex/Hampshire border betwen the sites of two Roman remains.

Being close to Portsmouth, many kings and queens from the Plantaganets to the Hanovers found it a convenient stopping place. More recently, royal visitors have included Princess Anne, Princess Alexandra and Prince and Princess Michael of Kent.

But this elegant stately home was first opened to the public in May 1985 at a glittering ceremony performed by actress Diana Rigg.

The original building was a royal hunting lodge, while Earl Godwin, the father of King Harold, used it as a base for his descents on the Isle of Wight.

The first recorded buildings on the site of the present 15th century chapel were built for Henry II.

He and his sons, Richard the Lionheart and King John, visited Stansted frequently during the end of the 12th and start of the 13th centuries.

During the 11th century, a hunting lodge was built at Stansted, probably for Roger de Montgomery, the first Earl of Arundel.

The Earls of Arundel continued to use Stanstead as a hunting lodge throughout the 13th, 14th and 15th centuries.

In the 18th century the house passed by will to the second Earl of Halifax.

There were various changes of ownership and by 1804 the estate had been sold to Mr Lewis Way.

In 1819 the chapel was reconsecrated at a service attended by the poet, John Keats. It is said to have inspired him to write the poem, The Eve of St. Mark.

He even completed part of another major work, The Eve of St. Agnes, while at Stansted.

In 1924, the estate was sold by Major Cecil Whitaker to Vere, ninth Earl of Bessborough, who was succeeded by his son, Frederick, the tenth and present Earl. He converted the old stables into a cricket tea room and the old laundry and bakery into a bathing pavilion.

In 1983, he handed his estate to a charitable foundation so that one day it could be made available to the public.

Steyning

While Sir Harry Gough was MP for Bramber, he had other things on his mind than affairs of state. Uppermost must have been one of the tenants of a house he owned in Steyning who was refusing to pay the rent.

Presumably in case he ever had to evict the recalcitrant tenant, Sir Harry, who was an MP from 1774 until 1790, fixed a plaque on the outside wall so as to leave no-one in any doubt who owned the house. Sir Harry Gough's House, as it is now known stands among the plethora of admirable buildings in Steyning.

There is the Georgian house where the poet W. B Yeats penned many of his later works. And there is the old grammar school, which was endowed in 1614, but occupied buildings built by a medieval brotherhood founded before 1388 and dissolved in 1548.

Steyning

The Chequers Inn has been standing in Steyning's High Street for over 400 years, and once used to be a coaching inn where steaming horses were changed and thirsty travellers refuelled.

The coach-house still stands at the rear of the pub as a reminder of those pioneer days of public transport.

Once Steyning had a bustling market with all the ingredients that these country town affairs used to offer.

It was to Chequers that local merchants would retire when the day's business was done. Inside, they used to take tally of the profits and then, doubtless, play a game of chequers, thus giving the pub its name.

There is record not only of the financial affairs of merchants, but also of the inn itself. In 1766 it was apparently insured for £500, and there is a bill of sale on display among the beams and ancient weapons as a reminder of an early transaction involving the Chequers in 1741.

But there was one happening which really used to get the feathers ruffled – cockfights.

This was something of a Madison Square Gardens of the cockfighting world.

One poster tells of a heavyweight contest staged when the men of Steyning – or rather their fighting birds – took on the men of Horsham and Henfield. The winner won five guineas and, presumably, a cheap fowl for Sunday dinner.

Now wagers are of a more respectable sort, the only chicken lies beyond broodiness in a frozen pasty, and memories are the strongest reminder of a chequered past.

Steyning

Court Mill, Steyning, is the sole survivor of four water mills in the village mentioned in the Domesday Book.

Court Mill, which originally belonged to Charlton Court Farm, is no longer used as a mill. It was converted into a house in 1929, and most of the machinery removed.

The original mill was rebuilt and enlarged over the centuries, and the oldest part of the present building is wood and plaster work, which is some 300 years old. There is some Georgian brickwork, while the front of the building is early Victorian.

The millwheel itself, used to help grind grain from the farm into flour, is dated 1872, and was made by Coopers of Henfield.

Streat

Lying in the heart of the tiny village of Streat, Streat Place adjoins a pretty Norman church on rising ground with splendid views of the South Downs.

The main facade, early Jacobean or late Elizabethan, is constructed of knapped flints under a Horsham slab roof and faces east.

The property is approached over a tree-lined drive leading to the main entrance, while the front door is set under a fine, three-storey porch with carved stone archway.

Streat itself has a distinguished place in Sussex history and was mentioned in the Domesday Book, 1086, under the name of Estrat.

At the time the manor belonged to William de Warrenne but by 1192 it had passed to Geoffrey de Saye, who was related to William the Conqueror.

During the reign of James I it was in the hands of Richard Evelyn, father of the diarist, John Evelyn, whose maternal grandmother, Eleanor Comber, was also a maternal forbear of later owners of Streat Place.

In 1595 the manor was acquired by Walter Dobell, who refashioned the earlier construction and external appearance of the house with the new east facade with additional projecting wings.

Oak panelling – now in the ground floor "Prince's Room" but originally installed in the room above – was added in 1610. This was in preparation for a visit by Prince Henry – Prince of Wales and son of James I – whose comptroller lived at Danny Park a few miles to the west.

Further alterations were carried out to the interior in 1745 and since then major reorganisation has taken place including additional staff bedrooms on the second floor.

During the last war the property was occupied by the Canadian Army.

Thakeham

Little Thakeham Hotel, in the heart of West Sussex, is one of the finest examples of a Sir Edward Lutyens manor house.

It was built in 1902, and although the house is less grand than some of its more famous English counterparts, its compactness is pleasing to the eye.

The local sandstone has weathered to make the house appear much older than it really is.

The character of a manor house has been retained and there are appropriate antique furnishings.

The central drawing room proves a talking point for visitors. It has the atmosphere of an Elizabethan hall, with its huge fireplace and minstrel gallery.

Casement windows in the 18in thick walls look over a garden created by Gertrude Jekyll, leading landscape designer in the 19th century.

Uckfield

Bridge Cottage in Uckfield is an aisled Wealden hall house, built between 1380 and 1420 and, judging by the high architectural standards, probably for a local person of some importance.

Much of the original timberwork remains to show it consisted of three sections – the service wing, the central hall and the solar wing.

The service wing, at the southern end, contained the pantry and buttery, and these ground floor storage rooms were separated from the main hall by a narrow cross passage.

The main living room was the most important area and formed a central hall with an open hearth and extensively decorated with moulded timbers.

The owner and his family would have sat at the northern end of the hall, which was furthest away from the smoke of the open fire and had an elaborately carved wall of oak panelling.

The house was built on a platform of clay brought to the site to provide a solid base, for the surrounding land was marshy.

The house remained almost wholly original until the middle of the 16th century when open halls became unfashionable. At the end of the 16th century the two brick chimneys were built, and the last section of the open hall was floored over.

Uckfield

Nutley Windmill, near Uckfield, is perhaps the oldest post-mill standing in Sussex today.

After 65 years of disuse it was restored by members of the Uckfield and District Preservation Society.

It represents the English post-mill in its basic early form, grinding corn for the local smallholders.

Very small in size, it is constructed wholly of wood and is a type known to have existed in the 12th century.

It is now unique in Sussex and the only workable one of its type in Britain.

This open-trestle mill is thought to have been brought from Goudhurst in Kent. Indeed, the mill is not recorded in Sussex until 1840.

Its commercial life ceased in 1908. The structure of the body had failed during the latter years of its working life.

Until 1971 it was shored up on steel joists and brick piers were placed under the sheers of the spout floor. The owners, Lord and Lady Castle Stewart, had these placed there to save the mill from collapse.

By 1972 the mill was working again for the first time in more than 64 years, even producing a small amount of meal. Volunteers had commenced restoration work three years earlier.

The whole mill is now in working trim. It received an Architectural Heritage Year Award in 1975. Restoration continued until 1981 when the mill became fully operative again.

Warninglid

The Half Moon at Warninglid can aptly be described as the pub that moved.

For the original half Moon started life in about 1500 at a now historic building at the southern end of the village.

But in about 1870 the building became a private house, and the Half Moon pub changed its location to a newer building at the northern end of the village high street.

Standing at the crossroads, the Half Moon looks like the typical Old English country pub, but in fact only dates from the 19th century.

When the pub moved to that building, other changes made themselves felt in the village.

For the original Half Moon also served as the village posting house, and when the pub moved, the old blacksmithy became the new post office.

Fortunately, the builders had the foresight not to build an out-of-place new house in the picturesque village, and so used the old bricks and tiles from the smithy.

Westmeston

Middleton Manor, Westmeston, dates from the early 1830's and has been a horticultural training centre for the last 40 years.

It began its life as a small, elegant manor house built by Mr H. C. Lane, and he bought his bride, Jane, daughter of Charles Lambert, to live there.

Over the years, however, the manor was enlarged to such an extent that few private owners could afford the upkeep. The house was constructed of white Horsham sandstone. This soon became damp so it was hung with the attractive red tiles which we see today.

During the last war the house was requisitioned by the Army, who used it as a holding camp before the Dieppe raid.

After 1945 the house was used by Plumpton Agricultural College to train students in horticulture.

Eventually it passed to East Sussex Social Services, who use it as a training centre for mentally-handicapped young people in country crafts and horticulture.

The headstones of the graves of horses belonging to the Lane family have been rescued from the woods, where the animals were buried and now they are on the verges of the front drive.

Mrs Lane had planted a tree in the back drive to mark her 70th birthday, and another in the south grounds to mark Queen Victoria's golden jubilee.

Westmeston

Parts of Westmeston Place, a brick, stone and flint-built Grade II listed manor house, date back to 1430.

Until the later 18th century, it was known as Westmeston Place Farm. It was enlarged around 1882.

In Tudor times, this partly weather-tiled house was owned by the Michelbournes and in one of the chimney pieces are two small shields, carved with the initials J.M., probably after John Michelbourne.

There is believed to be a priest's hiding hole in an upper room, while in the south side of the house is a mounting block. Rumours of a ghost are denied by the present owners.

The house is full of interesting architectural features, including Gothic exposed open windows.

The attic, which runs the length of the roof, was once the manor house's servants' quarters and houses some original wattle and daub construction.

Other notable 15th century features include roof beams of the period. Some of the original window frames also survive.

Winchelsea

Winchelsea Court Hall can lay claim to be one of the oldest buildings in the town – and in a place that dates from 1283, that's quite a claim.

But a quick glance at the depth and material of the walls and the rough hewn oak timbers, coupled with the architecture of the doors, all point to a very ancient building indeed.

Winchelsea originally lay on the east side of the Rother but was severely damaged by storms in 1252 and 1288. However, by 1280 Edward I had already acquired the manor of Igham and planned to build a new town there in the style of the French bastides and the Italian castelfrancos.

His purpose was not military but commercial, for the king planned to help the wine trade with Gascony by providing an up-to-date, workable settlement at this end.

But his town was never finished, and by the 14th century it was evident that the idea had not been wholly successful for holdings were lying vacant. There were also several French raids between 1337 and 1380, and in the reign of Elizabeth I the harbour silted up.

Historians have estimated that the Court Hall was built before Edward's plans for his "new" town were executed. But the conveyancing title for the building does not date back further than the reign of Henry VII.

He conveyed the royal manor of Igham, which included the Court Hall, to Sir Richard Guldeford – then bailiff of the ancient town.

Winchelsea

The Bridge Inn, Winchelsea, dates from the 15th or 16th century – making it a comparative youngster in a place that goes back to 1283.

Its original use was as a customs and excise house for Winchelsea was then a harbour for cross-Channel shipping, coasters and barges carrying coal.

In the time of Queen Elizabeth I, the harbour silted up, so it would seem the building's first working life was fairly short. It is not clear what then befell to the former excise house, but the owners have discovered that it has been an inn for at least the last 200 years.

Worthing

Famous visitors to Beach House, Worthing, have included King Edward VII, Arnold Bennett, J. B. Priestley and Sir Compton Mackenzie.

As its name implies, the Regency house, a stuccoed bow fronted villa, has gardens down to the sea. It was designed in 1920 by J. B. Rebecca.

For some years it was occupied by the Loder family, and between 1908 and his death in 1910 King Edward VII stayed there occasionally with Sir Edmund Loder.

In 1917 the villa was bought by the playwright Edward Knoblock. In 1920 he refitted the interior to the designs of Maxwell Ayrton.

This incorporated a lot of furniture from the sale of Deepdene in Surrey – neo-classical pieces by Thomas Hope.

Mr Knoblock's guests during his ownership included such literary luminaries as Arnold Bennett, J. B. Priestley and Sir Compton Mackenzie.

In the 1920s Worthing Corporation bought Beach House and its grounds, to provide facilities for bowls and tennis.